GOD IS GREATER

CELEBRATING

God's Goodness

in **EVERY**

SEASON

Bridging THE *Gap*

God is Greater: Celebrating God's Goodness in Every Season
Copyright © 2021 | Bridging the Gap

Publishing and Design Services | MartinPublishingServices.com

Contents

Section 3: God is Greater Than My Future

INTRODUCTION

As I reflect on the past two years and think about the numerous changes that surround us, at times it seems overwhelming. Yet when I consider the enormous seasons of transition I've experienced during my own lifetime, I'm so grateful God is in charge!

God is *greater* than any situation or crisis. He loved each one of us enough to die on a cross so we could experience his abundant life. And he is the same yesterday, today, and forever.

As I look back on the years, I think of all the times when God demonstrated how much greater he is than our circumstances would suggest. When one of our daughters was two years old, more than 40 percent of her body was tragically burned in an accident. Her life hung in the balance for months. In fact, we spent 22 years going back and forth to a hospital in Cincinnati, Ohio, as she recovered her health. Despite the challenges, God became greater to me and to our family.

Another time—39 years ago—we lost three businesses, our home, and everything except our kids and our souls. Even then, God was greater to our family.

And over the many years I've had the opportunity to lead Bridging the Gap, God has shown he is greater—even when I felt unqualified to accomplish his tasks. But he was and he remains greater than any situation that I've encountered, past or present.

As 2 Timothy 1:7 reminds us, "For God gave us a spirit not of fear but of power and love and self-control." (ESV) He desires for us to walk in freedom because his death on the cross set us free and gave us everlasting life. He wants you and I to be the woman he has called us to be.

He is greater!

Carol Lund
Director, Bridging the Gap

*"Now all glory to God, who is able,
through his mighty power at work within us,
to accomplish infinitely more than we might ask or think."*
—Ephesians 3:20

GOD IS GREATER THAN MY PAST

Day 1

Break Free
of the Comparison Trap

Faith Fitzgerald

Don't compare yourself with others.

Galatians 6:4 (ERV)

It was a warm, sunny spring day in the 1970s. My teenage sisters and I headed outside with our transistor radio in hand, swimsuits on, down the steps to our backyard with a large blanket to lay out in the sun. Our goal was to tan our fair, freckled Irish skin—compliments of our red-headed dad—and since sunscreen was not yet a consideration, we would put baby oil on our skin and lay on reflective blankets that looked like aluminum foil to get the sides of our legs tan at the same time.

My mom would emerge outdoors to hang up laundry on the clothesline, see us lying in the sun, and say, "Girls, get out of the sun. You are going to ruin your skin."

"It's okay, Momma," we'd reassure her. "We won't be outside for too long; we will be flipping over soon."

She would simply shake her head and tell us we would regret laying in the sun when we got older. Most days we kept good track of the time, but there were a few days we fried our skin to the point of getting blisters! At the time, tan skin, straight long hair, false eyelashes, frosty white or blush pink lipstick, and white go-go boots were fashionable. I often felt like I had been born in the wrong decade with my naturally curly hair and fair skin. By 13, I was caught up in the "comparison game." I wanted to fit in so badly I was willing to burn my skin if that meant I would look cool and be accepted.

To make matters worse, I was also caught up in the comparison game with my identical twin. Though she and I did not try to encourage competition with one another, many people would comment on whatever looked different between the two of us on a daily basis. If one of us happened to wear high heels to school and the other wore flats, people would comment on our height. If one of us wore clothes that fit more loosely, they would tell us who looked fatter than the other. Though we tried to be gracious and not let it show that it felt horrible to be the twin hearing negative comments, our facade didn't always work.

At that time in my life, I was not walking with Jesus, and did not have the best self-talk going on. I did not feel I was good enough and did not have a lot of confidence; I was extremely shy. Instead of knowing the Word of God and having confidence in who he says I am, I listened to the lies of the enemy.

However, the summer before I went to college, I began to walk with Jesus and read my Bible. As I did, I started to find my confidence in who God made me to be. I did not worry anymore about my fair skin or curly hair. I no longer felt like I had to fit in and be someone I was not; ironically, I had more friends than ever before. In my newfound, holy confidence, I knew the Lord had designed and created me just as I was, just as it states in Jeremiah 1:5: "I knew you before I formed you in your mother's womb. Before you were born, I set you apart."

The Lord has a different plan for each of our lives. If we embrace who God has made us to be, we can live a life of freedom. Even as an identical twin, I still have my own unique talents and gifts!

Today, I am on a first-name basis with my dermatologist. Over the past 25 years, I have had countless pre-cancerous spots frozen, burned, and cut off my body from all the years I damaged my skin from tanning without sunscreen and using good skincare. In the years that have passed since my baby-oil-and-aluminum-mat days, I have found freedom in walking with the Lord and reading his Word. I have learned how we are God's masterpiece. He created us anew in Christ Jesus so we can do the good things he planned for us long ago (Ephesians 2:10). As Psalms 139:14 reminds us, "I praise you, for I am fearfully and wonderfully made. Wonderful are your works; my soul knows it well." These are promises I began to believe and say to myself, and my thought life changed immensely.

Prayer

Lord Jesus, thank you for showing us who we truly are. Remind us daily of what you have called us to do and how our confidence is found not in how we look; it is only found in you. Lord, help us to avoid comparing ourselves with others. Help us to instead focus on who you have created us to be and how we can serve you and others.

Take It Further

Do you recall a time in life when you got caught up in comparison and your confidence was placed in the wrong things? How did you overcome it?

_____

_____

_____

Faith Fitzgerald is married and has a blended family of three adult children and one grandchild. She lives in the Twin Cities. Faith is the owner of Fitzgerald Recruiting, a professional search and contract staffing firm. With a BSBA in management, Faith has twenty-plus years of experience in talent acquisition management.

Day 2

Trivia or Truth

Andrea Christenson

Jesus wept.

John 11:35 (NIV)

As we sat in the sun eating ice cream, my children laughed as they recalled the puppet show from Vacation Bible School the night before. The skit featured a puppet who struggled with memorizing a passage of scripture. Seeing his frustration, his puppet friend offered to help out.

"Perhaps you can break it down into two parts," the puppet friend suggested. "What can you remember?"

The first puppet scratched his cloth chin. "Well, it was something about Christ crying."

I laughed along with my children at the puppet who couldn't memorize John 11:35, the shortest verse in the Bible: "Jesus wept." (NIV)

The answer to countless trivia questions and first choice for Sunday school memory verses, John 11:35 often gets a bad rap. I could see the humor in the puppet skit, but as I laughed, my throat closed around a lump. See, only a few days before the skit, my beloved grandmother had passed away. I was in the midst of writing her eulogy. Over the past few days, many, many tears had been shed by myself and my family.

Suddenly, "Jesus wept" wasn't just a trivia answer to me.

John 11:35 emerges right in the middle of the passage about the death of Jesus's good friend, Lazarus. Jesus was on his way to visit Lazarus and his sisters, Mary and Martha, in Bethany when he received the news that his friend had died. In the rest of the chapter, Jesus goes on to teach his disciples about the resurrection. He tells Martha, "I am the resurrection and the life. The one who believes in me will live, even though they die; and whoever lives by believing in me will never die." (John 11:25, 26 NIV)

Here is what I find so amazing about this passage of scripture: Jesus knew what came next. He knew he would stand outside Lazarus's tomb and order Lazarus to come out. He knew Lazarus would stand, shake off his grave clothes, and live. Furthermore, he knew that even if he did not raise Lazarus from the dead, his friend already possessed eternal life.

And yet, he wept.

In those two small words we learn an important truth—Jesus is human. He is subject to the same emotions we experience.

At the death of a friend, Jesus cried.

What comfort to know Jesus sympathizes with our grief. He sympathizes with us not only because he created us and loves us, but also because he, too, lost loved ones. The Bible doesn't recount all of Jesus's reactions to loss, but in this one instance, God sees fit to give us a glimpse of the divine heart and show us Jesus's sadness over the death of his friend. We can trust Jesus to be greater than our grief. We can trust him to walk with us through our valleys of shadow.

> *"For we do not have a high priest who is unable to empathize with our weaknesses, but we have one who has been tempted in every way, just as we are—yet he did not sin. Let us then approach God's throne of grace with confidence, so that we may receive mercy and find grace to help us in our time of need."* (Hebrews 4:15–16 NIV)

Although it did not erase the hurt of losing someone I loved, the thought of Jesus's full humanity—demonstrated through the tears he shed—brought peace to my heart. God knew what I was going through, and he was with me in the midst of my pain. Our grief need not be a lonely process.

Perhaps, like me, you've recently experienced a loss. Maybe you struggle to believe that anyone understands your grief. It could be that you are weighed down with your burdens and seek someone to shoulder them with you. If so, I pray that you find comfort in the shortest verse in the Bible: *Jesus wept.*

Prayer

Thank you, Jesus, for walking with us when we need comfort. We are grateful for your humanity and understanding of our grief. Amen.

Take it Further

Do you ever feel alone in your grief? What does it mean to you to know that Jesus cried at the death of a friend?

_____

_____

_____

If you are not experiencing grief right now, do you know someone who is and whom you could encourage with these thoughts?

_____

_____

_____

Andrea Christenson lives in Minnesota with her husband and daughters. When she is not busy homeschooling her girls, she loves to read anything she can get her hands on. She believes that a great loaf of artistic bread turns a meal into a masterpiece. Connect with Andrea at AndreaChristenson.com.

Day 3

Who He Says I Am

Jill Moltumyr

Do not conform to the pattern of this world,
but be transformed by the renewing of your mind.

Romans 12:2 (NIV)

It was an average Tuesday morning, filled with quick reminders for the kids and a rush to get out the door. Life had been busy—very busy—but I was determined to get to work on time. I was fussing at the kids and starting to lose my cool. My boss was an advocate for timely arrivals, and I still had a few things to finish before my first meeting. But I felt there was no way I was going to make it on time. I wanted to do a good job and show my boss that I was worthy of the job, but failure was once again on my doorstep.

I was consumed with thoughts of failing to meet expectations. This was just one more moment where I would fail. Fear and anger brought me back to the kitchen table of my childhood, unable to complete my multiplication tables or finish the peas on my plate.

Perhaps my boss would overlook my tardiness this time, but deep down, I felt I could never be the person others needed me to be.

Soon after that morning, I began to hear from others who had overcome thoughts of failure, and I was intrigued by their insights. They said that God does not see me as a failure. God says that those who come to him are his children. I've witnessed the way he loved his children throughout scripture, and see it now in the lives of these people. God says we are chosen and not forsaken. If you or I do something that is displeasing to him, he is gracious enough to show us and teach us how to live in a godly way.

How had I become so caught up with thoughts of failure that I couldn't claim the truth found in scripture?

Our past is such an unseen force in our lives. Though your thoughts and feelings are impacted by what has happened in your life, your past does not have to define your present or future. Only you and God can define what is to come.

In this world you will have trouble.
But take heart, I have overcome the world. (John 16:33)

God is not confined by what you have or have not done. He is not confined by what has or has not happened to you. He is limitless in power and grace. Your yesterday is forgiven and forgotten in his sight.

Today is a new day. Yes, your past may have informed how you see and react to a situation, but our sweet God is available to reform your sight and your thinking. Romans 12:2 says, "Do not conform to this world but be renewed in your mind." With God's help, you can begin today to reform your thinking.

The first step for me was to spend time in the Bible and in prayer. I learned about God's ways and let that transform how I saw people and situations. And I was inspired by how God deals with a person's past. Both Saul—now Paul—and Moses are terrific examples of renewed thinking. David, too, was impacted and transformed by his relationship with God.

Our God is in the business of transforming lives. If you have a way of thinking you'd like to change, try spending time renewing your mind by seeking God in the Bible and in prayer.

Prayer

God, I know you love me, your created one. You handcrafted me. My mind is full of thoughts and my heart is full of feelings that don't always line up with scripture and how you see me. Help me identify and redefine thoughts and feelings that are not true and not from you. Refine my thoughts. Help me see what you see in me. In the name of Jesus. Amen.

Take It Further

What situation popped into your head while reading this devotional?

_____

_____

_____

What area does God want to redefine in you today?

_____

_____

_____

Jill Moltumyr lives in Sweetwater, Tennessee, where she works as the associate pastor at her church. Jill's focus is on helping people know God, know themselves, and live out their purpose in life. She loves spending time in nature, especially when it's exploring the mountains of Tennessee.

Day 4

God is Greater than Our Hurt

Jody Stinson

He heals the brokenhearted and binds up their wounds.

Psalms 147:3 (ESV)

The deepest cuts are the ones left by those closest to us. For my family, that was the people in our home church.

As new missionaries, my family adapted to the changes of living in a new country that was vastly different from home. Everything was unfamiliar. We went from a cooler climate to energy-draining humidity. Our American house had air-conditioning and readily available hot water, while the one in Brazil lacked air-conditioning and hot water was only available through a strange electrified box in the shower. The safety we had always felt in our small town in the US gave way to the overwhelming presence of barred windows, gates, and padlocks that made every building in our new country feel like a fortress.

Hardest of all was the change from an active and involved church life to one where we struggled to even understand the Scripture references in the sermon. Making friends was hard when our grasp of Portuguese was limited to what we'd learned from language tapes. We missed the States, but we did have the support of our family and church family at home. I don't say church family lightly. We were very close.

But then lies were told about my family. Lies were believed. And the church I had trusted betrayed my family. I was in my early teens, and I struggled to understand. No matter how many times I heard what had happened, I wanted to know how people we had trusted—even loved—so much could do what they did. My view of the world changed. My ability to trust was permanently altered.

Healing took years and left some deep scars. But the climactic moment came when we finally returned home to our old church to demonstrate forgiveness. Walking in that door again was one of the hardest things we'd ever done. But Jesus didn't say to only forgive your brothers and sisters if it was easy. God was greater than our broken hearts.

Forgiveness is never easy, but God made certain Christians would have no excuse to not forgive. We are told, "Let love be genuine. Bless those who persecute you; bless and do not curse them." (Romans 12:9,14) We are shown forgiveness in action when our Savior on the cross said, "Father, forgive them, for they know not what they do." (Luke 23:34) With his example as our guide, we are commanded, "Be kind to one another, tenderhearted, forgiving one another, as God in Christ forgave you." (Ephesians 4:32)

If Jesus could ask the Father to forgive the people hammering nails into his hands and feet, what excuse do we have?

I don't think I would have chosen to experience what we did, and it did change me in both good and bad ways. Yet I clung to one verse that remains my favorite: "And we know that for those who love God all things work together for good, for those who are called according to his purpose." (Romans 8:28) I don't know who I would be, or who my family would be, if we hadn't experienced what we did. I can only trust that God in his infinite plan had a purpose for it and that the people we became on the other side were better equipped to do what God had called us to do. We were transformed to serve him in better ways.

But the story doesn't end there.

After ten years, we returned from the mission field. We ended up thousands of miles away in another state. After my grandmother became ill, we moved her to be close to us. A few years later, my grandmother passed away. It was too expensive for all of our family members to fly back, so only my parents were able to travel to bury her next to her husband.

Having moved several times and experienced the passing of friends, my grandma's funeral would be attended by only my parents, my aunt and uncle, and a few other family members.

But unexpected support arrived in the form of the pastor and his wife from the church that once hurt us so deeply. After reading about the funeral in the paper, they had decided to come and offer their sympathy.

Seeing them arrive meant a lot to my parents. The pastor and his wife hadn't come for my grandma—they had never really known her. But they had cared enough about my parents to show up for them at a difficult time.

Forgiveness is not a magic wand that puts everything back where it was, but our God is greater than our pain. He can restore relationships.

Scars will remain. But then again, my Savior also bears the scars of the sins I've committed.

Prayer

Dear Jesus, when we are hurt, may we remember you are greater than our hurt. When we struggle to forgive, may we remember you forgave us. Thank you for being greater. Amen.

Take It Further

Has a fellow believer ever wounded you so deeply you have struggled to forgive?

_____

_____

_____

Do you believe Jesus is greater than any pain or scars we might have?

_____

_____

_____

What next steps can you take today to let Jesus help you forgive that person?

_____

_____

_____

Jody Stinson writes with the goal of bringing readers hope through the Ultimate Hope. After an international upbringing, she continues to travel whenever she can. She works in marketing and writes freelance, including an ongoing devotional series for children that is currently available in thirteen languages.

Day 5

A New Understanding
of the Father's Heart

Jonna Meidal

*We know how much God loves us
and we put our trust in his love.*

1 John 4:16 (NLT)

I didn't grow up in the church. I therefore didn't like churchy things, and I didn't want part of something that—to me—smelled of mothballs and "buttoned-up hymns." Sorry. No, thank you. Someone else can take my seat.

Welcome to me as a teenager. I was a delight.

I cringe today at my selfish, misguided youth. I lived so completely for the world's approval, always wanting to look and appear perfect. I assumed that if I looked flawless, people would *see* me, *like* me, and therefore *love* me. But the more I strived for perfection, the lonelier I felt.

I wish I could go back to my younger self and say, "You are loved! God's perfect, so you don't have to be!" I've often wondered if my life would've turned out differently had I known these things . . . Would I have seen my parents' divorce for what it was and not a personal attack on my identity?

Would I have respected myself more around men? Would I have partied less and studied God's Word more? Maybe.

Some of these questions have kept me up at night. I've played the "should-haves" and "what-ifs" over and over again like a black-and-white rerun. But let's be honest, replays are never helpful. They never bring peace and rest; they only keep us locked inside our flesh instead of free in the Spirit (2 Corinthians 3:17).

But how do we move on? In my experience, absolution can only come when you fully understand and accept that God's love, grace, and healing are for *you*. Not someone more pious or "churchy." You.

I will never forget the first time I truly understood this concept. I was a new mom, exhausted yet so grateful to be on this journey with my newborn daughter. One night while rocking her to sleep, I felt intensely enamored with her tiny eyelashes and fingernails. *How perfect they seemed!* I realized in that moment that nothing—not death, lies, or betrayal—would ever keep me from loving her. She would be my heart forever.

Then BAM! The veil was torn from my eyes.

I could finally see that *this* was how God felt about me! *How had I missed it before?* I was speechless, humbled beneath the weight of his love. In that midnight moment, I finally understood my Father's adoration for me, his child . . . and so I started trusting him (1 John 4:16).

Trust is a hard thing to do, though. Especially if you've been hurt or abandoned by your earthly parents. But having confidence in God's love—regardless of what you've done, where you've been, or who you think you are—is the first step toward redemption. This truth leveled me. I had always believed love was something to earn or strive for but was finally internalizing something new—a perfect kind of love, one that was unconditional and could expel every last fear (1 John 4:18).

I needed the gospel badly in order to move forward because I felt terrified to do so. I knew my pain too well, could recite its every move like a bad dance partner. Victimhood had become a way of life for me, and freedom seemed illusory. However, once the veil had been lifted, I *knew* it was time to change. So like an infant, I slowly learned how to walk toward my Father.

This took time, of course. Shedding the weight of any historical burden is like peeling the layers of an onion: it's cumbersome, stinks, and often makes you cry! But God wants us to do it anyway. He just doesn't want us to do it alone.

I started seeking out friends who would help me navigate this new chapter of life. And guess where I found them: church! These women weren't "buttoned-up" or boring, either; they were real, trustworthy, and unphased by my past mistakes. They saw me exactly how God does; and in those pews of friendship, my life began to change forever.

If you, too, feel trapped by the weight of your past, I believe it's no accident you're reading this. God wants you to know that his love is for you and it's time to release whatever you're holding on to today.

Prayer

Father God, thank you for loving me even when I don't deserve it. Your love is incomprehensible, yet I accept it today with an open heart. I put my trust in your love and choose to believe that your perfect love will expel all of my fears. Thank you for being my protective Father who will never give up on me, no matter what might happen tomorrow and the day after that. I know you love me, and I love you too! Amen.

Take It Further

Think of something you are unnecessarily holding on to. Maybe it's something you did two hours ago or two years ago. Perhaps it was something done *to* you. Either way, I encourage you to stretch out your hands as an act of surrender and say, "I give this burden to you, Father. Thank you for taking it from me! I love you too much to hold onto it anymore."

_____

_____

_____

Read Psalms 54. Underline any truths that stand out to you, and then pray them out loud over your situation.

_____

_____

_____

Jonna Meidal is a mother to three wild and zany daughters and a wife to the funniest man on the planet. She is a writer, educator, birth doula, and travel junkie who can't get through the day without Jesus and popcorn. Learn more about her adventures at jonnameidal.com.

Day 6

My Miraculous Mat

MaryRose K. Thill

Then Jesus said to him,
"Get up! Pick up your mat and walk."
John 5:8 (NIV)

Have you ever thought about why Jesus told the paralyzed man to "pick up his mat"? What does he need his mat for? He's healed now! One day, I felt the Lord point out to me that the mat is a symbol of the man's testimony. A sign of his past restored.

When you hear the word "past," what comes to mind? For many, including myself sometimes, I instantly go to hardships—perhaps the things of which I'm not proud. For years, I tried to cover up my past or even make it seem better than it truly was. In Christian settings, when people would go around the room and share "their story," I often left out the big, painful events. I had the tendency to smooth it over to sound a lot like everyone else's story.

From the time I was a kid, I felt like an outcast; I wasn't like the rest. My mom died when I was only 12. I had the paralyzing tag of being "the abandoned one." So, I strived daily to fit in—to do whatever it took not to be left again. I was popular because I became good at conforming to my environment. My uniqueness was masked. I dared not share how I was really feeling. I became addicted to affirmation from everyone else, instead of finding it from within. I entered a period of time where I completely hung up my belief in God and found much more enjoyment in partying with lots of alcohol at bars and chasing boys for attention. I used to not share these details, fearing that I would be judged or would be looked at differently—nothing like the Proverbs 31 woman, that's for sure. I spent a lot of time not knowing how to articulate my story. *What do I share?* But I felt the Lord tell me, time and time again, "All. Share it all—don't hold back the details."

You see, if we know deep in our hearts that we are truly free from our past, we don't have any shame sharing the details. Our Lord Jesus paid the price on the cross and said it was finished. Our past is cleansed. Not fully sharing our stories discredits the miraculous, intricate details. Holding back for the sake of possibly being judged negatively by others just feeds fear instead of claiming the freedom Christ paid for through his sacrifice. Who knows, perhaps the details we consider messy are exactly what's needed to connect with someone in a way that helps *them* be set free. A chain reaction happens, simply because we were not afraid to share the details and declare our story boldly.

There is a reason all four gospels point out the paralyzed man who needs to pick up his mat and walk. The importance of publicly declaring your ashes-to-glory story is far greater than we realize. In the passage from Mark, Jesus was talking with skeptics and said, "Which is easier: to say to this paralyzed man, 'Your sins are forgiven,' or to say, 'Get up, take your mat and walk'?" Jesus heals the man and instantly everyone—including the skeptics—praised God. Where they once saw a paralyzed man, they now see a walking man. And the man's story didn't stop in that moment, because he picked up his mat and carried it like Jesus asked him to do. Others asked, *why are you carrying that mat—what's the story?* Of course, he had to tell them of his miracle. I imagine his response to their questions created a chain reaction of people wanting to know more about this healer, Jesus.

It's been seven years since I received ultimate healing from Our Redeemer and chose to pick up my mat and walk forward, following Christ. Putting my past behind me, but never forgetting it. I look at my mat in so many different ways. I remember all the desperate calls out to God at night. The memories of the agony I experienced lying there, feeling hopeless. Hoping for a change, for a miracle. Sometimes I look at my mat and my eyes well up with tears, realizing how gracious the Lord really was to me. Jesus chose *me* to heal that day. Because of that one moment, my life was forever changed—changed for the good. I look at my mat and am filled with gratitude, realizing all the things I have been able to see and do—the relationships that have been brought forth, because of this miracle moment.

Our Father longs for us to tell our redemption story. Our testimony pierces the hearts of skeptics and fills our own hearts with gratitude. The mat is a symbol that what was once stagnant is now alive. A marker of what has been redeemed. A reminder of, "God did that for me then; he will do it again." He will use you to perform the same miracle (for example, Peter tells a man to walk and pick up his mat in Acts 9:34). It is such a precious gift to share your story and see it click for others. As it was said in Mark 2:12 after the healing of the paralytic, "This amazed everyone and they praised God, saying, 'We have never seen anything like this!'"

Carry your mat with you boldly, with confidence. Don't hide it. Share the details and be ready for the Lord to use you to set others free. Remember those days on the mat were refining character days—days you can now stand upon and say, "I have truly been healed and set free. My Redeemer lives."

Prayer

Father, thank you for the past—for all the details that have gotten me to where I am right now. Thank you for setting me free in so many areas. Teach me, Lord, how to rise in complete freedom, to carry my mat wisely, and share boldly what you have done for me. Amen.

Take It Further

How much time do you spend thinking about your testimony? Take a moment and think back through the series of events. Write down a few areas of your life that were once paralyzing that are now active and free.

_____

_____

_____

MaryRose K. Thill is a fearless and creative thinker, an active doer, and an undeniable people person. She passionately enjoys cross-sharing positive strategies between the Church and the corporate world.

Forgiven

Nancy Holte

God's will is for you to be holy,
so stay away from all sexual sin.

1 Thessalonians 4:3 (NLT)

One of the things I like best about the Bible is that—other than Jesus—there are no perfect people. It's filled with mess-ups just like me. I don't know about you, but I like to have company when I mess up. That doesn't mean I want to drag anyone else down a path of sin with me; I just like knowing I'm not the only one who has failed.

For many years, I struggled with being attracted to men other than my husband. It's not something I'm proud of, and thankfully, it's an issue that God has helped me overcome. These days, if another man looks even remotely attractive to me, I remind myself that it's easy for someone to look inviting when I don't have to be with him 24/7 (or even 14/7)!

Anyone who has been married more than a day knows that all men (and women) have annoying little habits that can drive a person crazy. Burping, breaking wind (known in our family as "bottom burps"), snoring, taking over the sink when you're in the middle of brushing your teeth, and other annoying habits can rip the romance right out of a marriage. But the thing is that all men have the same annoying habits, you're just not around to witness them. It's easy for someone to look attractive when they are in a professional setting, just like it's easy for me to put my best foot forward when I'm out and about in the world.

With all that said, there have been a few times during my life when another guy has appeared to be far more appealing than my husband.

Several years ago, there was a man at our church who I was very attracted to, and I liked to think he was equally enamored because that's the kind of la-la land I lived in sometimes. Of course, I knew I was walking in sin and was annoyed it was happening. I had tried numerous things to get this man out of my mind—quoting scripture, diverting my attention when he was around—but nothing had worked. I finally decided to talk to one of our pastors' wives. She was a friend of mine, and I knew she'd have words of wisdom and still love me when all was said and done.

Here's the thing about sharing your sin with someone: Doing so brings it into the light. Satan likes to work in the dark, and when things are out in the open, he knows that he's sunk because God works best in the light. 1 John 1:6–7 says, "If we say we have fellowship with him while we walk in darkness, we lie and do not practice the truth. But if we walk in the light, as he is in the light, we have fellowship with one another, and the blood of Jesus his Son cleanses us from all sin."

Although my friend prayed with me and encouraged me, the following Sunday at church, I saw the man who consumed my thoughts, and my struggle to get him off my mind continued to plague me.

As I sat in my seat, I begged God to take the feeling away from me. I really did not want to be stuck in sin. It was then that I heard God say, "Nancy, when you get through this, I will use your story." At that point, getting through it seemed like a pipe dream, but at least I knew God was listening, and that gave me hope. Three days later, the friend I'd confessed to about my secret struggle called to ask if I would talk about purity to our moms group.

I thought, "Really, God? So soon?" But God knew that in planning for the talk, I would spend lots of time in his Word, focusing on ways to avoid sin. Sure enough, my feelings for the other man disappeared. In fact, I found him kind of annoying.

God has used my mistakes to remind me that he is greater than my sin. He doesn't want me to walk in the muck and mire any more than I want to be there. If I wander in the wrong direction, God doesn't abandon me, he finds a way to draw me back to him. And, when Satan tries to take me down by reminding me of my past mistakes, God is there to remind me of his forgiveness because he is always faithful.

Prayer

Dear Jesus, thank you for your faithfulness and your forgiveness. Thank you for helping me step out of the muck and the mire when I've gone astray. I love you and desire to honor you in everything I do. Amen.

Take it Further

Is there a recurring sin that plagues you? Try confessing it to a trusted friend.

_____

_____

_____

If you've sought God's forgiveness, do you believe he has forgiven you?

_____

_____

_____

Nancy Holte is a wife, mom, grandmother, author, humorist, and encourager who loves to encourage women in their faith walk. Nancy loves to travel, take pictures, and read—especially by the ocean. You can find her on Instagram, Facebook, and at www.nancyholte.com.

Day 8

We Reflect and Remember His Comfort

Rachel Booth Smith

Celebrate this Festival of Unleavened Bread,
for it will remind you that I brought your forces
out of the land of Egypt on this very day.
This festival will be a permanent law for you;
celebrate this day from generation to generation.

Exodus 12:17 (NLT)

Ten years ago, my 6-year-old daughter fell on the playground. The school nurse called, and Clara's teachers were concerned. But the combined factors of a snowstorm and her high pain tolerance kept us home that night instead of going to the hospital.

Around 2 a.m., the dog woke Clara up. She giggled, thinking it was silly. Yet I was filled with a thick dread, knowing how unusual it is for a dog to wake someone. I remember standing outside the kids' bathroom, waiting to put her back to bed, knots forming in my stomach. I still have trouble standing outside that bathroom.

A visit to the pediatrician in the morning led to an ambulance ride to the hospital. Doctors guessed it was a ruptured spleen; an MRI revealed a tumor encasing her kidney. A slip on the playground had torn the tumor and cancer cells were leaking into the lining of her abdomen.

The whiplash from those 24 hours was breathtaking. It still is, honestly.

There's a lot to grieve when you have a kid with cancer. Grieving her lost innocence. Grieving the loss of family equilibrium, mourning the forced exchange of stability for turmoil. The heartbreak of treatments that destroy cancer cells and healthy cells. Grieving the lost perception of control over my kids' future.

We were trauma zombies for months: radiation, chemo, surgeries, feeding tubes, ports, complications, physical therapy, occupational therapy. All the therapies. Every day was the same, yet every day was unpredictable. We made our plans in the morning, but cancer always got the final say. And everyone knows cancer is a jerk.

***

Do you have a day on the calendar that you dread? Maybe it's the date you signed divorce papers. Or when you got a phone call with devastating news. Or the day when you discovered a secret sin taking over the life of a loved one. What do you do on anniversaries marking the day your world turned upside down?

The Bible does not sidestep these anniversaries. God told the Israelites to remember how he brought them out of Egypt, a rescue rife with blood and desperate pleas for help. Christ told his followers to remember his sacrifice by breaking bread, just as his body—flesh and bone—were broken. Both the Exodus and the cross were violent stories of restoration.

> *"He took some bread and gave thanks to God for it. Then he broke it in pieces and gave it to the disciples, saying, 'This is my body, which is given for you. Do this in remembrance of me.'"*
> Luke 22:19

In our remembrance, there is solace in realizing that God does not deny the wounds that precede the rebuilding. Our family decided to mark the anniversary of that day ten years ago when we found out Clara had cancer. We determined that we would not forget how hard it was. As we watch 16-year-old Clara doing blessedly normal teen things, we are grateful we aren't still in cancer-land. Yet we remember that somehow our God carried her wounded body and our wounded hearts through that year because we are all still here and still standing. We can pause and remember that truth.

Have you encountered a tragedy that lingers? Not all hardships are public and not all traumas receive public support. Still, there is certainty in knowing that the heartache you grieve is fully known and seen by God.

With God's blessing, we recognize our grief with its depths and dimensions. In truth, to the extent that we express our messy emotions, we experience the miracle of his comfort. It's incomplete to celebrate only the good and not recognize the bad. In his command to remember, how very wise that God reminds us that hard and good things go hand in hand. So I—and you, too—can remember the exodus, the horrors, and the redemption. I remember the cross, the murder, and the salvation. And I remember cancer, its destruction, and his faithful comfort.

Prayer

Lord, help us to hold both the pain and the comfort as we remember who you are and how you have brought us through challenges and grief. We are thankful for your call to celebrate amidst complex emotions and bumpy roads. Amen.

Take it Further

Pause and reflect on an event that was difficult. Make two lists. On one list, name the griefs without editing yourself. On another list, ask God to show you where you found comfort in that season. Looking at both your lists, prayerfully reflect on God's provision within the trial.

_____

_____

_____

On the grief side of your list, which areas still hurt? Thank God for the healing he will continue to do this coming year.

_____

_____

_____

Rachel Booth Smith is a writer, teacher, and leader. When not working on her Master of Divinity at Pillar Seminary (class of 2023), Rachel enjoys sharing unique and scholarly biblical insights in a way that captivates listeners. She and her family live in Apple Valley, where their family soundtrack is Motown and 90s rap.

Day 9

Taking His Yoke
Upon Me

Renee Garrick

*"Come to me, all you who are weary and burdened,
and I will give you rest. Take my yoke upon you
and learn from me, for I am gentle and humble in heart,
and you will find rest for your souls.
For my yoke is easy and my burden is light."*

Matthew 11:28–30 (NIV)

Sometimes I've been a slow learner. Over the years, I've carried burdens that were not meant for me. And those burdens were heavy—really heavy. They brought no joy—only worry and frustration. Strangely, they all seemed like good ideas at the time. Think of the toddler who says, "Me do it my own self!" Then he proceeds to pick up (or attempts to pick up) the diaper bag stuffed with toddler essentials. What he doesn't know is that the weight of the bag is far too heavy for his little muscles. The huge bag is too bulky to wrap his arms around. The shoulder strap is dragging behind him. He doesn't understand that it's not his burden to carry. It's Momma's—or Daddy's. But when he receives praise for his efforts—his face brightens into a grin . . . until that strap trips him up.

Some burdens I've carried have stemmed from doing good works. However, when I was spiritually immature, I worked to impress people instead of glorifying Christ. Attention feels good, doesn't it? It's like the toddler feeling proud of "doing it my own self."

As newlyweds, my husband and I sought to serve our church body. With immature faith, we took on too much. At one point, we worked with the youth group, taught a junior high Sunday school class, and led the education committee. We also served as Sunday-morning greeters and even purchased altar flowers annually, marking our wedding anniversary. We looked good from a distance: we were leaders; we were involved. Then I was asked to serve in another capacity, as wedding coordinator. I readily agreed. I felt honored to be asked.

Looking back, I wonder whom God must have been nudging to volunteer before I took over each of those ministries. I believe someone—or several someones—missed out on the joy of serving due to my taking up those yokes. I know now that some of those ministries weren't my burdens to carry.

Certainly, wearing the wrong yoke didn't provide any rest for my soul. It made me stressed and tired; yet still I strove to do more—to be good enough to deserve Jesus's forgiveness. In my mind, it seemed as if I could never do enough, and I took on more and more until I was finally exhausted. However, in my immaturity, I didn't know how to back out of the mess I'd so happily charged into. My solution was a poor one. I dropped out of all my ministries in quick succession. I had to admit that I wasn't perfect, that I couldn't do it all. My husband, in a similar bind, did the same. And it was so embarrassing that we stopped attending services. We quietly slipped out the church door and didn't go back.

Thankfully, God forgives our mistakes, even when we fail so spectacularly.

It took us a while to go back to church. Eventually we each became involved in ministry again. After all, the Word tells me that I'm part of the body—and my church body needs this little pinkie toe. I have my part to do, but I need to take up the right yoke—not the one for the ear or the eye or the thumb.

As we mature in our faith, we gain wisdom to recognize more easily which burdens are indeed ours—and which ones aren't. I finally realized that I had to ask my heavenly Daddy to guide me.

Prayer

Father God, open my eyes to the burdens that are mine to carry—and the ones that aren't. Please remind me to drop burdens that aren't mine to bear so I can move ahead in the plans you have for me and fulfill your perfect will in my life. Amen.

Take It Further

Are you carrying burdens out of a sense of obligation or to earn your Savior's approval? To earn the approval of people? Set aside some time to examine your commitments, including ministry.

_____

_____

_____

Is it time to let something go? To pick up a new ministry? Ask the Lord about it.

_____

_____

_____

Renee Garrick is a longtime member of New River Assembly of God in Red Wing, Minnesota. After teaching English for 20 years, she launched a writing services business, the Grammar Queen. Her favorite editing and proofreading projects are devotionals, Bible studies, and personal history projects. Learn more at thegrammarqueen.net.

Day 10

God is Greater
Than My Storm

Shannon Velsor

But you, Lord, are a compassionate and gracious God,
slow to anger, abounding in love and faithfulness.

Psalm 86:15 (NIV)

"I'm not sure I can do this anymore . . . " were the words I spoke to my husband during one of the most difficult seasons of our life. We had a young church plant, a newborn baby, and a perfect storm of challenges that were blowing everything in our lives apart. Life in this season wasn't full of sweet, happy memories a mom cherishes with her newborn. Instead, it was a dark, lonely place I hope never to revisit.

A combination of postpartum anxiety and depression, along with very real ministry stressors, had created a windstorm that uprooted everything that mattered in my life, all at the same time. The challenges were so intense that I would sometimes imagine running away just to escape the pain. I even created a plan of where I would go and what I would do to be free from what I call "the dark night of my soul." I began to believe that my husband, children, and church would be better off without me. I couldn't get through a day without crying multiple times, and I felt they all deserved something or someone better than myself.

I often say I have two great testimonies in my life—my salvation testimony and my ministry testimony. My salvation story happened when I gave my life to Christ. My ministry testimony took place when I learned to trust him with my life. It's one thing to open our hearts to Jesus; it's another thing to trust him when you feel you've lost everything.

During this challenging season, a mentor shared that I would learn positive aspects of God's character I'd never know without such difficulties. Although it didn't seem possible, they ended up being right. Through my grief, I discovered a compassionate side of God I'd never known. Even though I was pushing God away, he never left my side. He poured out gifts of compassion, often arriving in the form of a person. I found myself surrounded by support I didn't know I needed, and one by one, God ushered voices of comfort, strength, and wisdom into my life. These were the guides that would ultimately shine light onto my path and help me stand firm in my faith. God used the gift of people to share words of encouragement, hope, and even correction to help me move toward the process of healing.

I also experienced the grace of God in profound ways. There was a never-ending flow of grace that helped me do things I couldn't have done on my own. Sometimes it was the grace to get out of bed; other times, it was the ability to stand firm in my faith, even while my knees were shaking. On darker days, Jesus helped me as a wife and mother to stay close enough to him that small pieces of his love would peek through the broken parts of my heart. He made up the gaps where I couldn't, and he protected me in my deepest times of vulnerability.

Through his compassion and grace, the Lord ushered me toward healing and transformation. My God was greater than the storms I walked through. Because of his goodness and kindness, he painted the banner of a rainbow over my life. This rainbow represents depth, knowledge, wisdom, compassion, and empathy. He turned my pain into beautiful colors of strength, love, and a deeper understanding of his goodness. I don't believe he caused those winds to blow into my life, but when he calmed them, it brought a strength that ultimately made me better than I was before.

Prayer

Lord, I thank you that your Word says you will never leave us or forsake us and that you will be with us until the end of the age. I pray you would be with us in our hardships and struggles, in our questioning and doubts. Pour your compassion, love, and grace over us today, and allow us to continue to stand firm in the faith. Amen.

Take It Further

Have there been times in your life where the storms felt like they could blow you over? What are the key areas that cause the greatest amounts of hurt or doubt (i.e. relationship struggles, financial hardships, physical health issues, fear, anxiety, unforgiveness)?

_____

_____

_____

Take a moment to reflect on areas where hurt or unforgiveness may exist. Allow yourself to forgive every person, by name, and call out forgiveness over situations that caused you pain.

_____

_____

_____

Shannon Velsor and her husband John planted "North Star Community Church" in Coon Rapids, Minn., in February 2013. They have two adventure-seeking boys, Aiden and Asher, who they've lovingly nicknamed "Danger and Smasher." They keep their mama in prayer and trusting God! Shannon wholeheartedly believes in the power of the local church to change the world and is passionate about serving it. She also claims to be a well-trained "Muay Thai" fighter, but she's really just into kickboxing with other middle-aged adults at her local Farrell's gym. Her self-confessed vice is Nitro coffee, and her biggest struggle is drinking just one.

Day 11

The Great Defender

Jaclyn Loween

How I love you, Lord! You are my defender.
The Lord is my protector; he is my strong fortress.
My God is my protection, and with him I am safe.
He protects me like a shield; he defends me and keeps me safe.
I call to the Lord, and he saves me from my enemies.
Praise the Lord!

Psalms 18:1–3 (GNT)

I have winced at the pain of being severely misunderstood. I have been the recipient of comments that degrade my age, gender, and intellect. At times I've felt cast aside—excluded. My voice knows the anguish of being unheard and silenced.

My wounds are a part of my journey, and not just those in the distant past. Some hurts are fresh and still sore to the touch. These battle wounds—these scars of the inside that nobody sees—they hurt. They threaten to bring me to my knees, white flag raised high.

And yet . . .

I am still standing. I am still moving forward. I even smile and laugh.

Am I being fake?

Am I covering up?

I don't think so.

Instead, who I am when God sees me is as real as anything else on this earth. And the person you see is happy to see you. The words you are reading are as true as they can be. Because somewhere along this path, I have come to believe—no, not just believe, rely on—the promise that God is my defender. I don't need to pretend I am not hurt. And I also don't need to fight back, get even, or form a case to justify my right to feel hurt, betrayed, or set aside.

Instead, I can press on, move forward, and live fully as the being God has made me to be; because he is my defender. He made me and desires more for me than I can even imagine of myself. I am his workmanship, created for good works. He not only knows what those works are, he jealously holds my heart and the work of my life in his hands.

And he is perfect and just. And I am not. So his methods, ways, and plans are always going to be better than any defense I could conjure up.

It isn't easy, this get-knocked-down-don't-defend-yourself life. But it is the only way.

It is the Jesus way.

It is the Paul way.

It is the way of the cross-stamped life.

Hurt hurts. Pain provokes a response.

But I am slowly learning that pain is not my enemy, hurt is not going to kill me, nor is a silenced voice punishment.

Rather, all of these lead me to an invitation to surrender my defenses to the Great Defender. These wounds call me to walk forward in full assurance of these truths:

He sees my heart.

He knows my thoughts.

He delights in me always.

He has given me a purpose and a mission.

I am slowly learning to live every day fully trusting and relying on the truth that I need not defend myself because God is way better at that than I will ever be.

Yes, I can and need to admit when I am hurt. I need to recognize when I am wounded. If I don't, I won't have a reason to go to the Father, asking for healing and restoration. And while he is tending to my broken places, I can rest in the fact that he is fighting the spiritual battles I can't see and building up a defense that protects my hope, secures my mission, and saves my soul.

Arrows are sent against all of us in an attempt to knock us off course, cripple our effectiveness, and kill the visions God has set in our hands to accomplish. And when those attacks come by way of the words and actions of others, it is hard to step into the med-tent to allow the Great Physician to dress the wounds.

But when you do—when you retreat—the battle doesn't cease. The other side doesn't win. Rather, the Great Defender takes on the weight of all that you've been exposed to. He is your Great Defender. He is your greatest defense.

Prayer

Lord, thank you for being my defender. Rather than relying on my own words or actions, help me to allow you to intervene on my behalf. I pray that I might find the joy, peace, and confidence that comes from you being the Great Defender in my life.

Take It Further

Meditate on Psalms 18:1–3 in order to see your present struggle as an opportunity to view God as your Great Defender.

_____

_____

_____

Jaclyn Loween holds a master's degree in teaching and learning and is the Christian Education Director and Middle and High School principal at New Testament Church and Christian School in Alexandria, MN. She uses her knowledge of how the brain learns and the truths of the Bible to help teens and adults understand the ways they are uniquely gifted and equipped to live a life of Christ-centered purpose. This spring, she published her first book, Go *& See. See all you have. Invest all you have been given*, a guide to help readers see their unique design and God-designed purposes. Jaclyn blogs about life as a wife, mom of four, educator, visionary, and avid runner. You can join her on her journey at jaclynloween.com and on Instagram @jaclynloween.

Section 2

GOD IS GREATER THAN MY PRESENT

Grace and Power
in Weakness

Becky Meyerson

And He has said to me,
"My grace is sufficient for you, for power is perfected in weakness."
Most gladly, therefore, I will rather boast about my weaknesses,
so that the power of Christ may dwell in me.

2 Corinthians 12:9 (NASB)

Have you ever avoided doing something because you felt you were not good enough, were too old, or lacked some qualification? That resistance is a common unhealthy thought pattern—and part of the enemy's strategy—to convince you that your weaknesses are too great to accomplish the task before you.

When I was 47 years old, I sensed that it was time to return to the classroom and *finally* get a pastoral license. God had dropped the word "pastor" into my heart in my early 30s, but more than a decade later, I thought that dream was long gone.

I naturally started forming a list of why this idea was too crazy to consider. I believed I was not good at writing. I also didn't know if I had the time and energy to commit to this educational adventure. Furthermore, I wondered if I would be embarrassed to be in a classroom full of 20-year-olds, which inevitably led me to question whether I was too old to learn.

My list of weaknesses and excuses almost took me out before I had even started! But with the encouragement of my husband and friends who recognized the call of God in my life, I began school that fall semester.

In 2 Corinthians 12:7–10, the apostle Paul asks God three times to remove a weakness he calls a thorn in the flesh. God didn't remove the thorn or replace it with one of Paul's expectations. Instead, he told Paul that his grace and mighty power works best in his weakness.

Often, like Paul, I look for a replacement for my weakness. I ask God for a quick exchange for the inadequacies I am experiencing. *God, will you switch my uncertainty to confidence and give me balance instead of perfectionism? Right now, Lord, I need capacity instead of overload, and patience instead of frustration. Will you give me quick answers so I don't need to ask for help or listen for your guidance?*

God responds with transformation instead of a substitution for my weaknesses: "My grace is always more than enough for you, and my power finds its full expression through your weakness." (1 Corinthians 12:9 TPT)

God's provision for every one of our needs arrives in his timing, in his way, and exactly when we need it. That way God gets the glory, not us!

I have found that three things will happen in your life when you celebrate your weaknesses, knowing you are filled with God's grace and power:

1. **You rise above your circumstances and feelings.**

   As I walked into the classroom on my first day, I could sense the young adult eyes on me and almost hear their curious thoughts. I shot a quick prayer heavenward as I found my seat.

When moments of weakness begin to occupy your mind, quickly call on Jesus and boldly come to the throne of grace to receive the help you need when you need it most. (Hebrews 4:14–16)

2. **You sense the strength of God as you move forward.**

Do not let your inadequacies hold you back as you fully trust God's work in your life. Surrender your weaknesses to God and then take a step forward, girded with grace and power.

You are set apart for God's glory, so you can entrust every endeavor into his hands. He promises to build you up and give you strength. (Acts 20:32)

3. **You are able to do more than you ever imagined possible.**

God's power is a work in your life, and he promises to do more than you might even ask or dream of accomplishing. (Ephesians 3:20) Dream big. Never give up. Press on.

As a daughter of God, you have the same privilege. Depend every day on God's grace and power in your weakness.

Prayer

Heavenly Father, I realize that I have been praying the wrong prayer. I have been asking you to remove my weaknesses and handicaps, when what I really need is to be filled with your grace and power. Forgive me for always looking for a substitute instead of transformation. I open my heart now and receive your sufficient grace and mighty power needed to move forward.

Take It Further

Make a list of the weaknesses that hold you back from moving forward on the path God has for you. Ask God what he thinks of your weaknesses. How are you experiencing his grace in the middle of each weakness?

_____

_____

_____

Now, put a large bold "X" through the list and write a prayer of declaration, praising God that your weaknesses lose their strength in the face of his sufficient grace and mighty power.

_____

_____

_____

Becky Meyerson encourages women to live a _Flourishing Life_ through her Rooted Bible Reading Plans and other resources that deepen and strengthen spiritual roots in God's Word. She loves to champion the woman who senses the seeds of growth and possibility but wonders how to cultivate that potential in her life. www.becky-meyerson.com

Day 13

Joy Over Heaviness

Carrie Curran

. . . the joy of the Lord is my strength.
Nehemiah 8:1 (NIV)

Joy. What does the word really mean? I think about it a lot and I want to be joyful, but sometimes, it's hard. As a little girl, I would pray over and over in my head, "Jesus, let your light, love, and joy shine through me." I wanted people to see Jesus in me, because all it seemed like other kids saw were my flaws.

There were days when I would tune out the world of middle school, and then there were days when I felt like a wet blanket was covering me that I simply couldn't escape. I felt helpless. Even now, there are days when it feels like there is a heavy weight pressing down on me. A lot of times, I get caught up in the weight of what the enemy is trying to do. However, there was a day when I realized what was happening and I proclaimed Jesus's love, light, and joy over the situation and the day before me. Almost instantly, what felt like a very heavy, wet blanket of sorrow, bitterness, and anger was lifted off of me. The cloud the enemy was trying to create was gone.

Choosing joy over heaviness, I believe, is a daily choice. Maybe that's why I prayed that truth over and over as a middle school kid. I didn't want the weight of what the enemy was trying to put on me to land and surround my emotions. Instead of the feelings of not being loved, wanted, or accepted, I wanted Jesus.

You are loved. Period.

No matter what type of day you are having, know this—You. Are. Loved. Let his wings cover you. Find shelter in the Almighty. The enemy will come, and he will try in every way to put a heavy, wet blanket on you. Don't let it land on you! Claim joy, love, life, freedom, happiness, and self-control.

You are a child of the King of Kings. And he wants what is good for you. His yoke is easy, and his burden is light.

> *"I will keep my eyes always on the Lord. With him at my right hand, I will not be shaken."*
>
> *Psalms 16:8*

Prayer

Jesus, sometimes I am weighed down by complaining, jealousy, weariness, and heaviness. Please help me proclaim your love, light, and joy instead. Help me to keep my eyes on you and you alone. Fill me with your joy and peace. I love you so much, Lord. Let your presence follow and fill me today. Amen.

Take It Further

For the next 30 days, take time to write down what brings you joy. It could be something that happened that day, a fond memory, or a pastime you enjoy. Write down the reason for your joy and thank Jesus for it. He created our innermost being, including the things that bring us joy.

_____

_____

_____

Carrie Curran is sometimes seen as a quiet introvert with not much to say. On one hand, she would agree. Yet hearing other people's hearts is a lifelong passion of hers. Carrie loves to learn and understand what makes people tick, including their passions. She is a wife, mother, and follower of Jesus. For the moments she feels less reserved, she shares her heart in her blog.

The Lord is My Provider

Donna Lewis

*. . . So there was food every day for Elijah
and for the woman and her family. For the jar of flour was
not used up and the jug of oil did not run dry, in keeping with
the word of the Lord spoken by Elijah.*

1 Kings 17:15–16 (NIV)

The move required more financially than we had anticipated. Everywhere we turned, a hand was extended, awaiting payment. The 1905 craftsman home we rented was beautiful but drafty; one heating bill eclipsed $600! In just a matter of months, all accounts were nearly empty. It was time for this homemaker to seek a paying job.

Early in July, I drove to an employment agency, took the tests, and filled out the forms. Seventeen years had passed since I left the workforce to rear my three children.

"Lord, only you know who would take a chance on this stay-at-home mom, with only part-time jobs on my resume. I trust you to provide."

Almost immediately, Kelly from the employment agency started calling me with job opportunities.

"Kelly, I'm sorry, but I can't start until August 12."

"Are you sure? This is a great opportunity."

"Yes, I'm sure. August 12." (This conversation was repeated a few more times.)

In late July, Kelly called again. "I know you said you can't start until August 12, but Donna, this is a fantastic opportunity: administrative assistant to the attorney at the nuclear power plant. The site is amazing and the benefits are fantastic."

"Kelly, listen. This move has been extremely hard on more than just our bank account. It's been difficult for my husband, my kids and—quite frankly—for me. We have a mini vacation scheduled the first weekend in August; then I need to get my kids ready for school. I simply cannot start before August 12."

Kelly sighed. "I hate that because opportunities like this don't come along often."

"I'm sure they don't, but I've prayed about this—a lot! And if this is the job God has for me, then it will still be available on August 12." Kelly reluctantly said goodbye; I bowed in prayer again.

Fast-forward to Friday, August 9. I dropped the kids off at school, had my quiet time, and had just begun my housework when the phone rang.

"Hello?"

An extremely excited Kelly was on the other end of the line. "Donna! You are not going to believe this."

"You have a job for me."

"Yes! And it's even better than the last one. It's the same company, only this job is at the executive offices downtown. Now, it's just a temporary contract, but I think it could work into a permanent job. And guess what? It starts Monday—August 12!"

After a phone interview with the supervisor, I was hired on a 3-month contract to manage a new database. The software was new and needed some tweaking, causing the three months to turn into five months, then into seven months. By that time, the manager had assigned me other duties. Despite the company-wide hiring freeze, she was able to garner approval from the CEO to hire me full-time.

After 17 years, two acquisitions, and four different managers, God called me to leave the company and start my own consultancy. Within two weeks of my resignation, my husband took a new job and we moved to another state. The move and my business start-up—followed by a pandemic—cost greatly.

Once again, all accounts are near empty. Am I worried? Not at all! *Jehovah Jireh*, The Lord My Provider, is still with me. He led us to this new home and to this new business endeavor. Therefore, he will see to it that my "jar of flour" and my "jug of oil" will continue to flow! I choose to trust him.

Prayer

Father, you are all I truly need. You supply good, important things. Forgive me for wanting lesser, unimportant things. Though you may not meet my greeds, you always meet my needs. Teach me to be content where you lead me and to trust you as my ultimate provider. Amen.

Take It Further

Do you have a pressing need (financial, relational, emotional, or other) with no idea how it can be resolved? Briefly describe it below.

_____

_____

_____

Be honest: Is it a need or a greed? If the former, give it wholly to God and trust him with it. If the latter, confess it.

_____

_____

_____

Now trust *Jehovah Jireh* to do what he does best!

Donna Lewis spent 17 years in talent development before starting *Live Up!*, a coaching and consulting business based on Philippians 3:16. She is a Precept Bible study teacher (30+ years), a certified coach with the International Coach Federation and Blackaby Ministries, and the author of *YOU-nique: Embracing God's Design for You.*

His Strength is Greater

Faith Fitzgerald

I can do all things through Christ who strengthens me.
Philippians 4:13 (NKJV)

It was a regular, busy day at work in which I was running from meeting to meeting. I got back to my desk around 12:15 p.m. I typically did not hear from my 17-year-old son, Bridger, during the workday but it appeared that he had called me several times while I was away from my desk and had left a message.

It was a beautiful Friday in January, the weather exceptionally warm—55 degrees—and my son's class had taken a field trip to a local ski resort. As soon as I saw his repeated calls, worry kicked in, and I clicked over to the voicemail right away. Bridger's voice was profoundly serious. He said that he had fallen a long distance and had heard his back break. I felt a surge of adrenaline run through my body as I immediately headed for the elevator to leave the building.

I called my son on my drive home. He had gotten a ride home from another student but needed me to get home as soon as possible to take him to the hospital. As I walked into the house, I saw my son on his knees with his elbows resting on the table, gently stretching his back. I lifted his shirt and could see a large bump coming out of the middle of his back.

Bridger told me that the large snow run was so icy from the warm weather that it launched him too far, and he missed a landing and fell more than 20 feet. He heard his back break as he hit the ground and he was so afraid he would be paralyzed. He said he yelled a cheer to heaven when he could stand up because he did not think he would survive. He was taken by ambulance to the hospital as I drove behind.

During the drive, I pleaded with God to restore and heal Bridger. I prayed for the medical staff that would be working with him and felt completely helpless as to what happened next. I was grateful God spared his life, but at the same time felt very frightened. *How could this have happened? How could the run be that icy and no one knew about it at the resort?*

After arriving at the emergency room, the staff began taking x-rays and scans. It was not long before I was told that my son had broken his back in two areas, torn ligaments along his spine, and compressed his vertebrae from the hard landing. As they were discussing surgery, my son began to feel his left leg becoming numb, and the staff got nervous about potential paralysis.

The following morning, Bridger was brought into surgery. It seemed to take forever. Family and friends joined me in prayer that morning. We all interceded for Bridger, pleading for God's grace and mercy to make my son whole again. The surgeon came out after a few hours and had an x-ray showing two large braces along the spine and eight titanium screws holding his back together. He told us that Bridger was going to recover almost completely, losing little mobility in his back going forward. We were so grateful for such a hopeful report.

During this ordeal, the verse that came to mind was "I can do all things through Christ who strengthens me." We would repeat it often, especially when the nurses asked him to walk the halls or do any activity that would send his pain over the top. I read Romans 8 over and over, reminding my son that nothing can ever separate us from God's love, that Jesus was with him, and that the same power that raised Christ from the dead was living in him so he was going to be able to overcome.

Bridger healed and recovered from surgery with no paralysis! God is so faithful and good.

Prayer

We praise you, Lord, for your faithfulness and goodness! We are forever grateful to you for the grace to endure any trial. Help us to always come to you first and fully place our trust in you, reminding ourselves that you are a loving Father with healing power.

Take It Further

When was there a time in your life you felt completely helpless to change a situation and you relied completely on God? How did that strengthen your faith?

_____

_____

_____

Faith Fitzgerald is married and has a blended family of three adult children and one grandchild. She lives in the Twin Cities. Faith is the owner of Fitzgerald Recruiting, a professional search and contract staffing firm. With a BSBA in management, Faith has twenty-plus years of experience in talent acquisition management.

Day 16

Receiving Peace
in the Night

Judy R. Slegh

Your mind will be clear, free from fear;
when you lie down to rest, you will be refreshed by sweet sleep.
Stay calm; there is no need to be afraid of a sudden disaster or
to worry when calamity strikes the wicked.

Proverbs 3:24–25 (The Voice)

Years ago, I struggled with a sleepless night. My son, Dustin, had recently had a DUI conviction, and I was fearful of what might happen with his drinking buddies while he was away for the weekend. As I lay in bed, fear, worry, and concern rose in me as I tried to pray. *Is he drinking too much? Will he drink and drive tonight?* He had promised to not drink and drive again. As I struggled with knowing how to pray for him, I was prompted to ask God this question, which seemed strange at that moment:

"Father God, I am concerned about Dustin. My mind keeps circling back to the past, but I need to sleep. What is causing this anxiety, fear, and worry?"

Immediately I heard, "Your upset soul is keeping you awake. It is not your spirit."

He chided me, saying, "Your soul (mind, will, and emotions) is racing out of control. Allow your spirit to give you sleep again by releasing your soulish thinking."

How do I do that? A Bible application search revealed Proverbs 3:21–26:

> My son, never lose sight of God's wisdom and knowledge: make decisions out of true wisdom, guard your good sense, and they will be life to your soul . . .

> Then each one of your steps will land securely on your *life's* journey, and you will not trip *or fall.*

> Your *mind* will be *clear,* free from fear; when you lie down *to rest,* you will *be refreshed by* sweet sleep.

> *Stay calm;* there is no need to be afraid of a sudden disaster or to worry when calamity strikes the wicked, for the Eternal is always there to protect you.

> He will safeguard your each and every step. (VOICE)

My mind was racing out of control, yet God counseled me regarding my son's situation. By praying for God's wisdom and knowledge, my mind could be clear so I could have a refreshing sleep. Wow!

I realized I shouldn't stress about the what-ifs regarding Dustin's choices. I forgave Dustin for what he had done in the past, for causing me fear and worry. As I prayed, my mind cleared. Within minutes, I fell into a sound sleep.

I thanked God in the morning for my peaceful sleep and for teaching me to seek his wisdom and knowledge. He made it clear he will always know the issues causing a lack of sleep.

I then pondered this question in prayer, "What should I have done if you, God, had told me my spirit was keeping me awake instead of my soul?"

Quickly I heard, "I can speak to your spirit and cause you to pray for Dustin. When prayer is needed, I will keep you up to pray. Then peaceful sleep will come at the right time."

Since I learned this, I've experienced some sleepless nights due to personal and family hardships in addition to painful decisions. I now catch myself with a simple prayer:

> "Father God, is the reason I am struggling to sleep due to
> my spirit keeping me awake or my soul keeping me awake?
> I need your wisdom."

I have learned to wait on the answer and respond quickly.

Sometimes I don't know how to pray when it is God speaking to my spirit. As I wait, emotions surface that confirm my concern to him. I sense God's heart for me, his comfort, and his promised actions in time. Romans 8:26 has helped me in this need to pray:

> *"In the same way, the Spirit helps us in our weakness. We do*
> *not know what we ought to pray for, but the Spirit himself*
> *intercedes for us through wordless groans."* (NIV)

God leans in to comfort and care for me as I feel weak. In time, the need to pray comes to an end so I can sleep, even as he continues to work on my behalf. I fall asleep, no longer feeling that I have to work anymore.

Prayer

Father God, sometimes I have trouble falling asleep at night. Fear, worry, and concern cause anxiety that keeps me awake. During those times, please guide me on how I should pray. Thank you for interceding on my behalf when I can't find the words. Thank you for the peaceful night's sleep you will provide after I pray. I love you, Lord. In the name of Jesus, amen.

Take It Further

Let's activate this by completing a sleep inventory. Take ten minutes to list concerns that have recently caused a lack of sweet sleep during the night.

_____

_____

_____

Ask, "Father God, is the reason I have been struggling to sleep due to my spirit keeping me awake or my soul keeping me awake? I need your wisdom." Wait for his answer.

"Lord, how should I pray? What should I release? I hand it to you and ask for peaceful sleep at the right time. In the name of Jesus. Amen."

Also, write the prompts above on a slip of paper to be kept handy when sleeplessness occurs.

Judy R. Slegh is learning and growing into a normal life again after a traumatic brain injury in June 2020. She is a former high school teacher, adjunct professor, author of _Help! I Have a Prodigal_ and provides inner healing prayer through Nephros Ministries (www.nephrosministries.org). Contact her at restoringtheruins@gmail.com.

God Is Greater
Than My Missteps

Renee Garrick

We know that in all things
God works for the good of those who love him,
who have been called according to his purpose.

Romans 8:28 (NIV)

One morning, after my husband Lance left for work, I started the laundry and bed-making before heading to my home office. A few moments later—such a surprise—a misstep. A twist of the ankle tossed me to the hardwood floor, where I landed squarely on my right elbow. My shoulder seemed to explode. A dislocation feels so . . . wrong. Strangely, it didn't hurt at first. *Oh, dear Lord, I need your help.* I had to get off the floor. By myself. Never so thankful for having regularly done my squats, I got to my feet by grasping the footboard with my good hand.

I had to get help . . . but my phone was downstairs. However, my computer was just across the hall. Cradling my awkwardly hanging arm, sitting at the desk, I realized just how right-handed I am. I left-handed an email—with only my index finger. Sending a note to my husband's two email addresses—both of which go directly to his phone—I had the forethought to send a copy to myself so that, when it arrived in my own inbox moments later, I could forward it to him again with only a few clicks.

Thank you, Lord, for that idea! I prayed that those four emails arriving simultaneously would get his attention: *help. i fell and hurt my arm.*

The next challenge was making my way downstairs. Of course, my stair railing is on the right so I couldn't hold it. Still cradling my arm, which had begun throbbing by then, I gingerly made my way down, counting the 16 steps. Just as I approached the kitchen, my cell began ringing. Lance assured me he was on his way. Thankful, I sat on the bench near the back door as the pain met me in waves. The only thing to do? Wait and pray.

But my mind spun with worry. Focusing on my injury, on myself, I battled the panic that threatened to take over. Suddenly I knew that I needed to focus elsewhere. Looking at myself, at my shoulder, I saw only bad. But when I looked to my Heavenly Father, he met me right there on that bench. The peace and comfort in that moment surprised me, and the more I prayed, the less pain I felt. How wonderful is his design, giving me adrenaline so the pain could wait. I've often said that when a situation seems like the worst thing, sometimes it's actually the best—because God can take any situation and make good come of it. In that peace, I was able to pray differently. I prayed that Lance would drive safely, that he would be calm. I prayed in advance for my medical team at the ER. I asked him for an opportunity to be a good witness for his goodness. I thanked him for a hospital only 10 minutes away.

Two hours later, heading homeward with a sling supporting my newly relocated shoulder, I was thankful. Not for the injury. Not for the pain—but for nurses and doctors. For x-rays and pain relievers.

Have you ever fallen? And I don't mean a physical fall. When have you blundered, slipped up, stumbled? Do you beat yourself up over missteps? Blame yourself for honest mistakes? Do you struggle to forgive yourself? Before I knew Jesus as my Lord and Savior, that's what I would have done. I'd have called myself careless, even stupid, for falling and injuring myself.

What a relief it is to shift the focus in a different direction and simply trust God in difficult times. "We know that in all things God works for the good of those who love him, who have been called according to his purpose." (Romans 8:28, NIV) Peace can come, even in an emergency—when I remember those words.

Prayer

Father God, thank you that you are always with me. I'm so grateful for your presence in difficult times and that you work all things for my good. Please remind me to look to you first—in every situation. In Jesus's precious name, amen.

Take It Further

Do you handle your own stumbles and honest mistakes by being hard on yourself—or forgiving yourself? Take a few moments to list both the areas where you need to forgive yourself and the ways that God has worked things out for good in your life.

_____

_____

_____

Renee Garrick is a longtime member of New River Assembly of God in Red Wing, Minnesota. After teaching English for 20 years, she launched a writing services business, the Grammar Queen. Her favorite editing and proofreading projects are devotionals, Bible studies, and personal history projects. Learn more at thegrammarqueen.net.

His Goodness
in Uncertainty

Nancy Raatz

Give thanks to the Lord, for he is good;
his love endures forever.

Psalm 118:29 (NIV)

First, I lost my sense of taste. My favorite lentil soup was tasteless mush. The next morning, I felt exhausted. COVID-19 had hit our home. My husband and I numbered cases eight and nine in our county, early positives in a worldwide pandemic.

We were exposed at a large gathering before large gatherings were stopped. When the wisdom to wash your hands and use hand sanitizer were the only ideas for "staying safe."

Our local health department dictated strict protocols to follow at home. Precautions, rules, and news changed daily over the week I spent in bed.

We were the first cases many knew about. Friends and strangers prayed for us, fearing the worst. In these bedridden days, the presence of Jesus became so real. I didn't fear but leaned into "be still and know I am God."

Jesus invited me into his presence. He drew me to know him. He taught me of his goodness.

The virus ran its course. My ability to taste and sense of smell returned, and slowly over the following weeks, my strength returned. I thought I had conquered the mountain, but there were many difficulties ahead.

The virus grew worldwide, and the tension of the year grew personally and publicly. Interpersonal issues arose. Disappointments abounded. The year ended with a personal loss that felt like a betrayal. Where was God in this?

Scripture declares he is right with me. As a teen, I had memorized Psalm 139. This scripture demonstrates how God sees and knows us intimately. It displays his deep love for us, but it scared me. Instead of intense care, I saw a God who searched me and watched my ways to correct me and find my faults. He was harsh and strict. This was the God I knew.

I grew older and God began to teach me the truth of this passage, a truth I'm still learning. He searches what I do because he is a Father who delights in me. He is for me. He walks with me every moment of my day and celebrates who he created me to be. He is there with me in each of those moments.

We know all moments in life are not celebrations. Life brings sickness and death, betrayal and broken relationships. We have days that are hard. Sometimes those days turn into weeks and months. We wonder if God still sees.

He does. He sees the anger, the tears, the hurt, and he holds them. He accepts my raw emotion, never telling me it is too much for him. Still, he delights in me. I am his daughter. He loves that I bring every moment to him, the good and the bad. He extends his hand of kindness and compassion and displays his goodness.

In a time filled with so much difficulty, he taught me his goodness. It came when friends dropped by with meals and when another said, "You are on my mind. I prayed for you today." It came when a friend reminded me that

I'm worthy of good care, and in the kindness of strangers paying it forward at the drive-through. He spoke to me during Bible reading and in the early hours of the morning through God-given dreams.

I have learned that although life is not always easy, God is good. He willingly proves this day after day. He is a God who sees me, cares for me, and is good to me.

In the stillness of his presence, may we know he is good. In the busy rush of the day, may we know his love is rich and deep. May we understand he sees our insecurities, our hurt and pain, and he can handle it. May we truly grasp his incredible goodness demonstrated on our behalf.

Prayer

Lord, thank you for your goodness. Thank you that you demonstrated that first by sending a Savior to redeem us. May we be aware of your deep care for us in our good days and in our bad, and may we delight in you as you delight in us. In the name of Jesus. Amen.

Take It Further

Take ten minutes and name ways you have seen God's goodness in your life. Thank him for that.

If it is difficult for you to see God as a loving and caring God, ask him to reveal this past to you in the days and weeks to come.

Nancy Raatz is a lover of Jesus first and foremost. She walks this out as a wife, a mother, an ordained minister, and a missionary. She loves to cook and provide hospitality to anyone who comes through her door.

Trusting in His Love After Loss

Miki Speer

God is our refuge and strength, an ever-present help in trouble.
Therefore we will not fear, though the earth gives way
and the mountains fall into the heart of the sea,
though its waters roar and foam
and the mountains quake with their surging.

Psalms 46:1–3 (NIV)

When I lost my amazing mother to cancer at age 13, I gained an unexpected worldview shift: The people we love most can die at any moment.

What a dark, depressing mindset change: To go from the sunny disposition of a young Christian who truly believed God could do anything—like heal a mother despite her stage-4 diagnosis—to the dark realization that just because he *can* doesn't mean he *will*. Perhaps you have experienced a similar shift in thinking.

It's no surprise that the decade after my mom's death was a complicated period of loving the Lord, my church, and all the blessings he had given me, while simultaneously keeping everyone (and everything) an arm's length away to make sure I didn't get *too* attached.

When we lose someone we love, we sometimes also lose our trust that God will protect us. When that trust is gone, we stop letting people in and stop getting our hopes too high because we don't want to watch them shatter on the ground again.

As hard as it is to feel sometimes, God still provides for us even when we walk through the unthinkable. For whatever reason, this world is not pain-free, and I am slowly but surely learning that we aren't supposed to strive for that ideal. In fact, it's just the opposite. We are called to love and to love deeply, and yes, that means there will absolutely be pain in our future.

But we must ask ourselves, "Do I trust God's command to love more than my need to prevent pain? Do I trust that if I follow what he says and open my heart to the immense beauty of being close to someone (or something), God will provide for me if it gets taken away?"

For me, choosing to say "yes" every morning has changed my life.

Scripture says that even when "the earth gives way," when our loved one dies, when we lose our job, when a friend betrays us, when our big prayer doesn't get answered, etc., we do not have to go into that fearful self-protection mode. Because God is greater than our pain and he *will* provide for us even in that terrible place.

We will never have all the answers. Leaning into love will not always be easy. But even though our hearts may shatter over and over again, we may walk with the assurance that we will be cared for and our lives will continue to receive, and give, blessings for the rest of our days.

Prayer

Dear Lord, forgive me for the many ways I try to protect my heart from pain. You know the scars of my past and the fears of my today. Lord, I give them all to you. Remove my desire to live life pain-free and replace it with the confidence to live faith-full. I trust that you will take care of me, that you have not forgotten about me or my desires, and that your command to love is worth the potential pain. Thank you for loving me deeper than I can possibly imagine. Amen.

Take It Further

Who have you lost in your life?

_____

_____

_____

How can you trust harder, love deeper, and be more vulnerable with those you love today?

_____

_____

_____

Miki Speer is a musician, author, and talk show host who is passionate about helping people lean into their own grief and learn how to help others with theirs. Check out her grief songs and workbook at mikispeer.com.

He is Greater Than My Season

Mykelti Blum

. . . for I have learned to be content whatever the circumstances.

Philippians 4:11 (NIV)

I sit on my front porch while drinking a cup of coffee, snuggle in a blanket, watch the last bit of rain drip off the trees, and take a deep breath. It has been awhile since I've been able to breathe and be still. I feel peaceful for the first time in months. As I do, I find myself wondering why the anxiety, why the chaos, why the confusion? That saying, "when it rains, it pours," comes to mind.

Many of us have been in a place where life feels a bit numb. We can't focus on what's ahead, feeling overwhelmed by the present.

Sitting in that moment of difficulty, I find myself hearing that still, small voice: "In seasons of challenge, I am not absent. I have never been closer. My plans are greater than anything you can imagine. Find peace in me."

Just this reminder brings me contentment: A reminder that in every season, good or bad, we serve a God who is in control, the great I AM. He is our provider, healer, father, and the gracious giver of hope. But learning to be content, to be satisfied, is not an easy task. It's easy to find contentment when everything is going right. We sing praises to God, thanking him for his faithfulness, his blessings, and his provision, but when things take a turn, do we continue to celebrate his goodness?

Our discontented hearts are always looking for the next best thing. We compare ourselves to others and struggle to find acceptance for where we are at now. Or we might be in a season of pain and hardship, and the idea of contentment makes us physically laugh out loud. We wish things were different. We sometimes wonder, *Is God still good? Is God even there?* So how do we learn to be content in *every* season?

As I sit on my patio, it all comes to me. It is the realization that God is present in every season. God is greater than our hard seasons. He is greater than our frustrations, our insecurities, and our feelings of inadequacy. God is always working and always faithful, even if his plans are different from what we ask and consider as being faithful. And God's plan for our life is far better than anything we could come up with ourselves. In all seasons, hold on to the truth that his goodness is a firm foundation.

In our present moments, we remember that God is the great I AM. That whenever we are hurt, lonely, overwhelmed, or feeling afraid of what the future holds, we can sit in our current present and know that God is greater than anything that comes our way. When we acknowledge all of this, we can find strength, peace, and contentment in every season.

Prayer

Lord, I pray that when I experience trials, I can find contentment in knowing that you are a God greater than any battle I may face. Help me to find rest in your faithfulness and remember that your plans for my life are better than anything I could come up with on my own. Help me to find peace in your goodness and to celebrate you in all my seasons. In the name of Jesus. Amen.

Take It Further

Do you currently feel content in life? Do you find yourself trusting God in all seasons, good or bad?

_____

_____

_____

Spend this week journaling about all the areas where you see God's faithfulness in your life.

Mykelti Blum is a licensed social worker, speaker, and founder of Heart of the Brave Ministry, which includes the Coffee with Kelti podcast. Mykelti believes in the power of vulnerability in sharing your story to encourage people in life. You can connect with Mykelti on heartofthebrave.com, or on Instagram @mykelti_blum.

Day 21

Embracing His Heart

Judy R. Slegh

"But I have prayed for you, Peter, that you would
stay faithful to me no matter what comes.
Remember this: after you have turned back to me
and have been restored, make it your life mission
to strengthen the faith of your brothers."

Luke 22:32 (TPT)

Recently, I have struggled to regain my life. In June 2020, a bicycle accident caused skull fractures and brain bleeding that required brain surgery. Part of the temporal lobe in my brain was removed. For the next four days, I experienced a coma with no brain function. My family sent out prayer requests for God to heal me.

I don't remember the accident or the first three weeks afterward. For four weeks in the hospital, I received physical, speech, and occupational therapy. I felt anger, despair, frustration, depression, and hopelessness while in the hospital. My mind swirled with questions, "Why did God allow this to happen? Where is he now?"

Due to certain restrictions, my family and friends participated in daily Zoom sessions where they prayed for me, read scriptures to me, and encouraged me.

I didn't feel a strong draw to embrace the prayers they prayed or the scripture they shared during this time. I enjoyed the time but felt disconnected from believing their confidence in my healing progress.

After returning home in July, I struggled with emotional confusion along with sleepless nights. Being sad, mad, devastated, depressed, and helpless became familiar emotions. Before the accident, I was involved in three ministries. My focus was to help and support others. I felt empowered to do God's work. Now, I felt disqualified.

At first, I couldn't read the Bible. It was too much work for my mind. Slowly, I was able to read. I also found a daily devotional that addressed my conflicted emotions. Though I told myself "I'm supposed to be a believer," I couldn't embrace God's truth.

Friends would pray for my mind to heal so I could recover my emotional health. At first, their prayers would ricochet off of my brain when they were finished. This frustrated me as I experienced little change. I knew it was due to the brain injury. Slowly it started to come back. I wanted my emotional health and relationship with God restored. Over time, as I continued to pray, I started to feel some emotional relief.

One day, I read Luke 22:32 where Jesus said, "But I have prayed for you, Peter, that you would stay faithful to me no matter what comes. Remember this: after you have turned back to me and have been restored, make it your life mission to strengthen the faith of your brothers." (TPT)

This was significant to me. As I prayed for understanding, I felt Jesus say, "Judy, I have prayed for you to remain faithful no matter what comes. After you have turned back to me and have been restored, you will strengthen the faith of others." This stunned me. I realized that Jesus understood my situation, my lack of faith, and the emotional turmoil I had experienced. As I reflected more, I sensed Jesus speaking:

"For days, Peter cried, just like you, Judy.

For days, Peter was mad and sad, just like you.

For days, Peter felt alone and abandoned, just like you.

You are now on the path of restoration. Many others need to hear the same message."

As I thanked Jesus for this message, I felt hopeful, more at peace, and close to Jesus again. I realized he has a plan.

God knows the difficulties we face in life today. He spoke to me. He wants to speak to you. If you are waiting for faith to come back, Jesus is praying for you. Your strength will be restored. Let's pray.

Prayer

Jesus, the complexities of faith have been challenging and gripped me with emotions that need healing. It has made me wonder if you are involved in my life. The truth of scripture says you are praying for me, like Peter. I choose to turn back to you. As I come back, my faith will be restored. I speak agreement to this. Help me to be strengthened to help others as I receive healing emotionally, physically, and spiritually. In the name of Jesus. Amen.

Take It Further

In what area of your life could you use restoration?

_____

_____

_____

What is something you could do today to maintain or gain back your faith in Jesus?

_____

_____

_____

How could you strengthen the faith of those around you after being restored?

_____

_____

_____

Judy R. Slegh is still experiencing the full restoration of her brain and body. She has now resumed inner healing prayer sessions through Nephros Ministries (nephros-ministries.org). It is her desire to know more of what her ministry will involve as she heals. You can contact her at restoringtheruins@gmail.com.

Section 3

GOD IS GREATER
THAN MY FUTURE

Day 22

His Mercies are
New Each Day

Brittany Jones

And the God of all grace,
who called you to his eternal glory in Christ,
after you have suffered a little while,
will himself restore you and make you
strong, firm and steadfast.

1 Peter 5:10 (NIV)

"It won't always be this way." She let the words roll off her tongue confidently, as if she believed them *for* me.

The truth is, I needed her to. Experience had shown me that suffering lasted longer than I ever wanted it to, but I still knew she was right—even if I wasn't sure how to believe it for myself yet.

As I sat in my therapist's office, not fully aware of my surroundings, let alone what my future was going to look like, I felt hopeless. An eating disorder had ravaged my life, and I felt as though it had almost disqualified me from doing anything significant or great.

My therapist looked at me with a warm smile and reminded me again, "It won't always be this way, and God has a purpose for your life."

I had heard about "God's purpose" for most of my Christian walk, but it takes on new meaning when you feel like you are literally walking through the valley of the shadow of death. Purpose seems elusive when you feel like a disappointment and a failure. Yet there I was, sitting in her office, being reminded that God still had purpose for me.

"Me?" I questioned. "How can he have a purpose for me?" I felt like I had let God down, so why would he use me?

I was a pastor's wife, a worship leader, a mom, and a Christian. I wasn't supposed to struggle with an eating disorder. Mental illness and imperfections didn't fit into the job description, at least that's what my perception had always been. I had only seen the best of people at church and in leadership.

At that moment, I realized I had a choice to make. I could lean into "my purpose," knowing that God's plan was so much bigger than the journey of recovery, or I could stay where I was, steeping in shame and guilt and letting the pain of mental illness keep me bound in secrecy. With the help of professionals, I chose to lean into purpose.

Over the last few years, I have witnessed the goodness of God in ways I had never experienced. When you decide that you are worthy, and that there is glory on the other side of pain, you push through the hardships and discover the way in which God offers you grace for the journey. That doesn't mean the process is always easy or that suffering doesn't exist. But God offers us new mercies every single day. (Lamentations 3:22)

One of my favorite verses is found in 1 Peter 5:10: "And the God of all grace, who called you to his eternal glory in Christ, after you have suffered a little while, will himself restore you and make you strong, firm and steadfast." In other words, it's like God is saying, "It won't always be this way."

Our suffering won't last forever, and in the process, God will refine and prepare us for a greater purpose.

Prayer

Dear Jesus, thank you that although suffering and pain are part of the journey, hope resides on the other side of suffering. Give us grace for the journey as we choose to lean into your purpose. Help us to welcome new mercies, new grace, and a lasting hope as we recognize that you are greater than all we face. In Jesus's name, amen.

Take It Further

Are there circumstances in your life that have tried to rob you of purpose, perhaps because the season has lasted longer than you imagined it would? If so, take a moment to journal and consider these questions:

What circumstances in your life have hindered you from choosing to walk in God's purpose?

_____

_____

_____

Where have you seen God's goodness in the midst of the journey?

_____

_____

_____

What three things can you celebrate before you get to the position of fully walking in God's purpose?

_____

_____

_____

Brittany Jones is a mother of two girls, Jalynn (10) and Jayda (7) and proud wife of 12 years to Travis. Together, Travis and Brittany lead Motivation Church in Richmond, Virginia. After growing up in the inner-city, poverty-stricken community and suffering many years of childhood abuse and mental illness, Brittany's desire is to reach all people. Her story is one of trials and triumphs. Brittany's hope is to inspire and encourage people to look back to the redeeming work of Christ in the midst of their brokenness. She is dedicated to motivating and encouraging others with a message of hope.

Day 23

Trusting Him
in the Freefall

Erica Horyza

Let the beloved of the LORD rest secure in Him,
for He shields him all day long
and the one the LORD loves rests between His shoulders.

Deuteronomy 33:12 (NIV)

"Am I finally doing better this time?" I prayed with a laugh as I realized the trial I'm enduring is a familiar one. Though the circumstances are vastly different, the test is the same: Will I trust God in the middle of uncertainty?

Several times in recent years, I've found myself in the same uncertain middle—having moved on from the security of one place but not yet having arrived at the next. There was the time I found myself unexpectedly pregnant—twice. And, oh yeah, every time I've flown on an airplane in my entire life. I'm rather adept at trusting God before takeoff on the nice, solid, reliable ground, and I'm pretty great at trusting him again once that plane lands, but in the middle? From the moment those wheels lift off until they safely land, I am a wreck. Relax and enjoy the view? Never.

Here I am in the middle again, except a plane would feel secure at this point. This feels more like a free fall in between the rungs on a trapeze, groping for the next bar while blindfolded.

Three months ago, my husband went to work as he had done faithfully for sixteen years, then came home after lunch with his box of belongings. Jaw agape, I froze as he uttered the words, "I quit."

"You quit? Your steady, lucrative job of 16 years? During a pandemic? Three weeks before the most tumultuous election of our lifetime? Not when we had one kid, or even three. But five. We have five children! What are we going to do?" I thought, fears instantly running rampant in my mind.

"I clearly felt God prompting me to quit," he explained.

How does one argue with that?

I spent the next four days sobbing almost continually, full of grief on so many levels. The moment felt like the loss of the foundation on which everything else in our lives stood. Income does tend to be necessary for most things; however, it wasn't only financial concerns that plagued me. I was afraid of having to move and uproot our kids. I felt a relational loss as many of our closest friendships had been cultivated through work. I even felt the loss of my identity. Apparently, my value had been tied to being married to someone with a job. Who knew?

The allegorical airplane of my life had not only lifted off, but I was at cruising altitude and someone had pushed me out!

A good friend recently shared about her experience skydiving. According to her, I never have to go. I've already experienced it all: the complete terror of free fall, mouth hanging open, unable to breathe, flailing in terror. Could I relax and enjoy the view? Never.

But she did.

She didn't enjoy the free fall, but after the instructor deployed the parachute, she started to rest as she realized her parachute was holding her steady. She was secure. This gave her the opportunity to recognize the beauty of what few get to experience—both the breathtaking view and the rush of being held fast even in the midst of what appeared to be danger.

Was there a metaphorical ripcord I could pull to not only survive my free fall, but also enjoy it?

Yes. It's the ripcord of trust. In the middle of uncertain times, our trust in Almighty God is what allows us not only to survive, but to thrive. Just as my friend's reliance on her parachute enabled her to enjoy the view, our recognition that Jesus is greater than our circumstances and that he holds us steady enables us to live the abundant life he promises, even while in the midst of uncertainty. We can gracefully experience the ambiguity of the middle, resting secure in his promises. And if we trust him, we, too, can experience the unique beauty and rush of being held fast by God's hand, even in the midst of what appears to be danger.

I don't know how long I'll be suspended in mid-air. Only God can control when my feet will be planted in firmer circumstances, but I get to control when I pull the ripcord. At any moment, I can choose to trust. I can choose to believe that God has a plan and that, although my circumstances may not be ideal, he is good. He is worthy. He is working. He can be trusted.

As I choose to trust that Jesus is here in my present circumstances, I can let go and trust him with my future. In that place of trust, I find an intimacy in him holding me steady. Instead of dangling in the atmosphere by my lonesome, I'm nestled securely in this sweet spot between his shoulders, on the ride of my life. And from this place, soaring through the uncertainty with the King of Heaven's armies, I can finally relax and enjoy the view.

Prayer

Lord, help me to choose to trust you in the middle of my uncertainty. Help me sense your firm grip even as I feel like I'm in free fall. As I learn to rely completely upon you, help me find beauty and freedom through surrender. Help me find intimacy with you, fully internalizing that I am your beloved and that I can rest securely with you.

Take It Further

What are some promises from scripture that you can fully rely on during uncertain times? Write your favorites in a journal or a file online to easily access when those times arrive.

_____

_____

_____

Erica Horyza is learning to embrace God's grace in the chaos of homeschooling and raising five children. She loves sharing her journey with other women in the hope that they, too, will find grace and freedom in Jesus. Her heart is happiest around a table full of food with a house full of guests.

He Can Be Trusted With My Worry

Jayne Poli

"But when he, the Spirit of Truth, comes,
he will guide you into all the truth.
He will not speak on his own; he will speak
only what he hears, and he will tell you what is yet to come."

John 16:13 (NIV)

When I was in junior high during the early 1980s, I received a Magic 8 Ball as a Christmas gift. I had requested this popular item and was thrilled when I received it. Using the Magic 8 Ball on the school bus was a very popular activity that elicited lots of giggles. I found myself using it in my bedroom, as well. It gave incredible insight to important questions like, "Should I wear my parachute pants today?" There was something so comforting about asking something beyond myself to make my decisions.

Even at that tender age, I knew decisions could affect my future in unforeseen ways. The ability to blame my choices on the Magic 8 Ball gave me a feeling of freedom from consequences that was very enticing. (Of course, I now know seeking any foretelling of the future from anyone or anything other than the Lord is wrong.)

I have often worried about how my decisions could impact my future. I have fretted about what I should be doing with my life. I worried about what could happen to my loved ones if I did or said the wrong thing. I worried I was not fulfilling my God-given purpose for me. I worried I had already finished my purpose and was just taking up space while I waited for heaven. I worried I was missing the boat by doing something I thought was a good idea but was not God's best for me. In other words, worry has often been a constant companion I've had to guard against.

After I committed my life to Jesus, I began to better understand how Jesus holds my future and knows all. He directs his children on the way to go. He goes before us to prepare the way for our future with him. As John 14:1–2 reminds us, "Don't let your hearts be troubled. Trust in God, and trust also in me. There is more than enough room in my Father's home. If this were not so, would I have told you that I am going to prepare a place for you?" (NLT)

Worry is a byproduct of wrong thinking. It's even classified as sin. Luke 12:28–30 tells us, "But if God so clothes the grass, which is alive in the field today, and tomorrow is thrown into the oven, how much more will he clothe you, o you of little faith! And do not seek what you are to eat and what you are to drink, nor be worried. For all the nations of the world seek after these things, and your Father knows that you need them."

Trusting Jesus as the Good Shepherd is the antidote for worry. There is no need to worry about the future when Jesus is your shepherd. We know he always has our best in mind. John 16:13 reveals the secret to being confident in our future, "But when he, the Spirit of Truth, comes, he will guide you into all the truth. He will not speak on his own; he will speak only what he hears, and he will tell you what is yet to come."

As we trust in Jesus's direction for us, he leads us to the abundant life both here on earth and in heaven that he promised. It has taken years of daily time with Jesus to learn his voice and distinguish it from my own desires. In John 10:27, Jesus says, "My sheep listen to my voice, I know them, and they follow me." The more we recognize his voice, the more we trust it. The more we trust in his daily care of every detail of our lives, the less we will worry.

As Romans 12:1–2 reminds us, "I appeal to you therefore, brothers, by the mercies of God, to present your bodies as a living sacrifice, holy and acceptable to God, which is your spiritual worship. Do not be conformed to this world, but be transformed by the renewal of your mind, that by testing you may discern what is the will of God, what is good and acceptable and perfect." (ESV)

Prayer

Lord, speak to us today. Show us clearly what you would have us to do. Help us to take this time to be still in your presence and listen to your voice. We know your will for our lives is good, pleasing, and perfect. We trust you with the future. Amen.

Take It Further

Ask the Lord to show you some plans he has for your future as you read your daily scriptures over the next few weeks. Journal what you feel the Lord is sharing with you during your prayer and Bible study. Ponder and pray about how you can step out in faith to bring his plans for you to fruition.

_____

_____

_____

Write down the things you are worried about today. Ask the Lord to show you scriptures that address these worries. Ask God to speak to you as you wait to hear his voice.

_____

_____

_____

Jayne Poli has credentials with the AG, is a registered nurse, a mother of three daughters, nana to four adorable grandchildren, and a speaker, writer, and artist. She loves to laugh and hopes to spread hope and joy in all of her artistic expressions.

What Can Man Do to Me?

Sandy McKeown

"The LORD is on my side; I will not be afraid.
What can man do to me?"

Psalm 118:6 (BSB)

My husband signed us up for informed delivery with the United States Postal Service. Through this service, we get an email of the deliveries we will be receiving each day.

So when it landed in my inbox, I saw the letter I had been waiting for—with apprehension—was finally arriving.

I had requested that the mortgage insurance company pay off the mortgage after my husband's unexpected death. They had already turned me down once. But their reasoning didn't seem accurate, so I resubmitted.

My long-awaited answer would be in the mailbox that afternoon.

I had appointments to keep and errands to run, so I left the house and forgot about the impending verdict until I was about a mile from home. Would they say "yes" this time? Would the premiums I had paid for years pay off?

Would I be able to get one more item checked off the burdensome to-do list since my husband had passed away ten months prior?

I drove slower as I neared the house—and the mailbox. My mind began to conjure up all the different scenarios of what may come:

They're probably repeating their "no."

I'm just going to need to be more careful with money.

Dreams have been shattered before; I can do this.

Then I realized I was being fearful. I needed to stop that impulse.

Dear Lord, please help me!

As I turned into the driveway, the radio station I was listening to changed songs. Zach Williams' "Fear Is a Liar" started playing.

Sometimes our Lord is so quick to answer.

Even as Zach sang words cautioning that fear would steal my happiness, I opened the door of the mailbox and spotted the letter from the insurance company on top of the pile. I snatched it out of the box and ripped open the envelope, scanning past the "niceties" in the first paragraph. My eyes found what I was searching for, in essence: *We need more medical records.*

Ugh! I didn't get a resolution. I felt deflated after getting myself all hyped up; literally, I had worried over nothing.

I still wanted this issue solved.

But I didn't get the resolution I sought. That is, I didn't get it in *my* timeframe.

The next morning, as I continued my study of Psalms I'd been clinging to during this new season, I came across a verse that seemed to be just for me. It was almost as if I heard: *My daughter, this one is for you today.*

I read Psalm 118:6: "The Lord is with me; I will not be afraid. What can man do to me?"

Yeah, what can man do to me?

My Lord has promised to take care of me, that he will provide for me, and that I have nothing to fear. Why do I keep forgetting his promises?

When the Israelites crossed the Jordan River, the Lord instructed them to place rocks at the edge of the water so generations would know what the Lord had done for them. *Maybe I need some rocks*, I thought.

The Lord gave me a really good man for 41 years—this truth is something to remember! My rocks are framed pictures of that good man in my living room.

I have five healthy kids—something for which I'm very grateful! My rocks: More framed pictures in the dining room.

Seven grandchildren have been added to the family tree, and two of our kids haven't even started their families yet. More framed pictures on the walls, proverbial rocks for me to remember God's goodness.

As I began to look around my home, I realized there are other rocks I've overlooked, like the notes scrawled in my Bible that I've owned for more than 40 years.

In the margin near Isaiah 26:3, "You will keep in perfect peace him whose mind is steadfast, because he trusts in you," I noted the date a friend referred me to that verse. *The date she directed me to this verse was just three months before my husband died.*

Near Matthew 25:21, ". . . Well done, good and faithful servant! You have been faithful with a few things; I will put you in charge of many things . . . " I noted: *Get on with the job! It's our responsibility to use our God-given gifts and abilities.*

And in John 21:7, "When Simon Peter heard that it was the Lord, he put on his outer garment . . . and plunged into the sea." I noted: *Recognize the Lord, surrender and jump in!*

When I page through these "rock-solid" reminders, the fear that had harassed me faded. They're small rocks, but the ripples provide comfort.

Thanks for the reminders, Lord. You are with me. This I believe. Today, through your strength, I'm resisting fear and trusting you for whatever may come next.

Prayer

Lord, help us to place the situations that cause fear into your hands. We trust you. We know you know best. Your will be done. Amen.

Take It Further

When you're totally being honest with yourself, what do you fear?

_____

_____

_____

What can you do to remind yourself to focus on God instead of your fears?

_____

_____

_____

Sandy McKeown, a speaker and author, has contributed to several anthologies, including *I Choose, Audacious Love, Tenacious Hope, Adamant Faith* and *Habits of Success*. Her first book, *Some Miracles Need a Mom,* will be available December 2021. Sandy lives near four of her seven grandchildren, where she laughs often without fear of the future.

Day 26

Grace for
Our In-Between Seasons

Bri Slegh

He who has begun a good work in you will [continue to]
perfect and complete it until the day of
Christ Jesus [the time of His return].

Philippians 1:6 (AMP)

Recently, I've found myself in a season of "in-between," unsure where I'm going, yet no longer where I used to be. It started when our landlord abruptly sold the place my husband and I rented, forcing us to move in with my in-laws. At the same time, my coworker quit, thereby doubling my workload. I also started to feel God nudging me to leave my job, and my husband began to feel called to leave his job and potentially move out of state.

I've found this season can do two things: It can shake you and paralyze you with fear of the unknown, or it can get you excited and expectant for what is ahead. Reflecting on my own season, I couldn't help but notice the parallels to two different stories in the Bible.

The first is the story of Israel's exodus from Egypt. The Israelites had been enslaved for 430 years when God led them out of Egypt and they made their way through the wilderness to the promised land. The Israelites had left the familiar and were headed into the unknown. All they knew was that God had a plan and he was going to lead them. Though they struggled to hold onto hope, God met them with his mercy and his faithfulness. He constantly led them by a pillar of cloud by day and a pillar of fire by night (Exodus 13:21), he provided food and shelter (Exodus 16:4), and he set them up with the blueprints of how to live by providing the Ten Commandments (Exodus 20:1–17).

The Israelites' journey is a reminder that God will provide. He will show me the way through this season of uncertainty, no matter how long the "in-between" lasts. Even when I'm weary, tired of waiting, or doubt the destination, God's mercy is new every single day. He is faithful. Though the Israelites' journey was longer than it should have been because they forgot God's faithfulness, he still saw them through to the promised land.

Our Father is so merciful and patient. When we struggle to hold onto hope, when we experience doubt or confusion, God meets us in those places. He is not surprised, and his love is not dependent on our feelings. He certainly is not deterred from helping us get back on the path again if we desire it. Scripture tells us, "He who has begun a good work in you will [continue to] perfect and complete it until the day of Christ Jesus [the time of His return]." (Philippians 1:6 AMP)

Whenever I find myself in a place of doubt, I remember this truth: I can't possibly trust God to take care of me if I don't know him. Knowing Jesus by spending time in his Word is the only way to build a relationship and foster trust.

Knowing the Father's heart helps us when we doubt or wonder, but it can also help us remember to turn to him when those worries turn to fear. A great reminder of this truth is the story of the disciples traveling with Jesus across the sea of Galilee. Jesus had said to the disciples, "Let us cross over to the other side" (Mark 4:35)—meaning to the country of Gadarenes— so off they went by boat into the sea. As they were crossing the sea, they encountered a storm. The disciples were fearful and quickly woke Jesus to help as he was sound asleep. Jesus said to the storm, "Peace, be still!" and the wind immediately calmed (Mark 4:39 NKJV). Next, he asked the disciples, "Why are you so fearful? How is it that you have no faith?"

The word "fearful" in this sentence is actually from the Greek word *deiloi,* which translates to "cowardly." Jesus meant that the disciples had lost their courage, fearing that the storm was more powerful than God. But just as Jesus's response demonstrates, we have the authority to overcome our fears through God's power. As 2 Timothy 1:7 states, "For God has not given us a spirit of fear and *timidity,* but of power, love and self-discipline." Just as Jesus asked his disciples why they were fearful, he asks us the same questions: "Why are you so intimidated? You have authority here to tell the wind and waves to stop. I have promised that we will go to the other side and I keep my promises. When fears arise like the wind and waves, respond with my authority: 'not today, Satan.'"

Friends, we have the opportunity to partner with God no matter what storms we face. His plans for us are good (Jeremiah 29:11). Even in our season of in-between, his reminder to us is the one he gave Moses as he was crossing the wilderness on his way to the promised land: "So be strong and courageous! Do not be afraid and do not panic before them. For the Lord your God will personally go ahead of you. He will neither fail you nor abandon you." (Deuteronomy 31:6 NLT) Though I'm still in this season myself, when I get discouraged about where I'm going and feel lost in the darkness, I declare this verse and it reminds me that I don't need to know the path before me. All I need to know is he is with me, he is going ahead of me to clear the pathway, and before I know it, I will find myself in the promised land.

Prayer

Father, we come before you expectantly, excited to see you move in our in-between season. Fill us with your power, your love, and your sound mind for the journey ahead and guide us with all wisdom so we always know the next step to take. Help us to shift our perspective to praise for you. Thank you that you are good and faithful in all seasons. In Jesus's name, Amen.

Take It Further

Reflect on a past season of life. How did God show himself as faithful to you? What encouragement does that give you regarding how he will show up in your current season?

_____

_____

_____

Pick a section of the book of Psalms and write down the promises and attributes of his character that you find.

_____

_____

_____

Bri Slegh has a background in human resources and is a recruiter for Animal Humane Society. She is passionate about helping women know Jesus intimately and pursue all he has called them to be without fear. She has volunteered on prayer teams with her church and with Bridging the Gap and is honored to be this year's project manager for the *God is Greater* devotional.

Day 27

Trusting Him
in the Adventure

Julie Fisk

Do you see what this means—all these pioneers who blazed the way, all these veterans cheering us on? It means we'd better get on with it. Strip down, start running—and never quit! No extra spiritual fat, no parasitic sins. Keep your eyes on Jesus, who both began and finished this race we're in. Study how he did it. Because he never lost sight of where he was headed—that exhilarating finish in and with God—he could put up with anything along the way: Cross, shame, whatever. And now he's there, in the place of honor, right alongside God. When you find yourselves flagging in your faith, go over that story again, item by item, that long litany of hostility he plowed through. That will shoot adrenaline into your souls!

Hebrews 12:1 (MSG)

It was a warm, sunshiny day in late January as we stood on a gently curving path leading us toward the Sedona Red Rocks. As we approached the base of Bell Rock, a giant rock that vaguely resembles a bell but looks, to me, like a double scoop of reddish ice cream plopped onto the hard earth, we couldn't help but notice the tiny, ant-sized people standing at the very tip-top of the rock.

Seeing those foolishly intrepid souls, my daughter turned to us and excitedly asked if she could *pretty please* climb to the top, too. Sharing a glance, my husband and I started quietly discussing whether or not the climb was doable and, more importantly, safe.

We strolled as we talked, and as I drew near to Lizzie, I heard her talking softly to herself. Intentionally tuning in to her one-sided conversation, I suddenly realized that she was muttering the following over and over:

"No risk, no fun. No risk, no fun. No risk, no fun."

My momma heart stuttered momentarily at her words, as I realized yet again that my daughter sees the world in a way that sometimes makes me a little nervous but also proud. I often wonder how God will use her love of adventure as part of her individual Hebrews 12 faith race, her calling, and her unique journey as she does her best to love God and those around her throughout her lifetime.

Faith in God can feel risky. We are almost always required to step outside of our comfort zones and trust God without knowing the details of how it will work out. Jesus was countercultural, and we are often asked to be the same—and that can feel both scary and hard. Yet God is good: a father who guides, protects, and delights in walking his sons and daughters along the cliffs and the narrow, twisting paths instead of along the broad avenues that are safe, predictable, and followed by so very many others.

We need not travel to far-off lands in order to go on an adventure with God. Perhaps he is asking you to invite an international student from a local university to experience an American holiday meal with your family, or to finally introduce yourself to that neighbor you still haven't met and invite them over for s'mores over a backyard fire. Maybe he is nudging you to start a book club or quietly meet a financial need of someone you know. Faith adventures can be found in our backyards, around our dinner tables, along the youth sports sidelines, and in our work spaces.

The question is whether or not we are going to answer his call on our lives, saying "yes" in faith and trusting that God will make our paths straight. Friends, saying "yes" to God, even when it feels scary—especially when it feels scary—is always, always worth it.

Prayer

Heavenly Father, thank you for inviting us to step beyond our own understanding and trust you with our whole hearts. Thank you for your faithfulness in response to our obedience. Thank you that your plans are bigger than anything we can begin to imagine when we respond to your invitation. We pray for peace over the hearts, families, and homes of every woman standing on the edge of her comfort zone, contemplating her "yes." In Jesus's precious name, amen.

Take It Further

What slightly scary thing has God been asking of you? Tell a friend and take one step forward in that new adventure this week.

_____

_____

_____

Julie Fisk has authored six books, including _The One Year Daily Acts of Friendship_ devotional for women and _100 Daily Acts of Friendship for Girls_. Together with her co-founders of The Ruth Experience, Julie connects with thousands of women online, encouraging their faith races to love God and love others.

Day 28

Wishes, Thoughts, and Prayers: Prayer is Greater

Marie West

But when you pray, go into your room,
close the door and pray to your Father who is unseen.
Matthew 6:6 (NIV)

Wishes. As every calendar year begins, we find ourselves wishing people a happy New Year. We send a greeting card to wish someone a happy birthday. You may even think of the Disney movie where the genie grants three wishes to Aladdin. Generally, we use the word "wish" as a hope or a desire that somehow things may go well. Though we can be very sincere in our wishes for good things, in the end, a wish does not have any power other than producing warm fuzzies for a moment.

Thoughts. It's the same with thoughts. We may hear the phrase, "our thoughts and prayers go out to the family at this difficult time." Sending "good thoughts" has value when shared with the person you are thinking about. "I've been thinking of you lately so I'm calling," is an encouraging word. These can release feel-good hormones in the bloodstream that improve physical and mental health. Proverbs 17:22 tells us a cheerful heart does good like medicine. Saying "I'm thinking of you" tells a person they are loved and cared about. The power in a thought, then, is in its encouragement.

Prayers. How much greater is prayer? In Matthew 6:9–13, Jesus tells his disciples how to pray in what is referred to as The Lord's Prayer. Take a look:

> *"Our Father in heaven, hallowed be your name, your kingdom come, your will be done, on earth as it is in heaven. Give us today our daily bread. And forgive us our debts, as we also have forgiven our debtors. And lead us not into temptation, but deliver us from the evil one, for yours is the kingdom and the power and the glory forever. Amen."*

We are in need of help in our relationships, decisions, and dealing with spiritual forces around us. The Bible makes it clear that there is none more powerful than God to help us. Prayer is a conversation with God, asking him who is greater than any situation for help.

I moved during 2020, and like a lot of people, I downsized 45 years of accumulation. I came across a handwritten note that was given to me, a fresh-faith believer at the time, by an older woman who barely knew me. The note was a prayer and prophetic word written as a love letter from God. That she took the time to pray for me, write it out, and give it to me is a treasured memory. It is still so treasured that the note did not go out with the trash.

Years later, I paid it forward using prayer. A friend in need had a request, so I typed out a prayer and messaged it to her. Later she told me that all week she went back to that prayer and repeated it over and over. It gave her peace in a difficult situation.

A wish gives a warm feeling inside. A thought gives us encouragement. A prayer gives us access to the almighty God.

Prayer

Lord Jesus, your disciples asked you to teach them to pray. We have your words of instruction recorded in scripture. Thank you for that guidance. My eyes look to you as I bring my needs and the needs of others to your throne, because there is power in prayer. Amen.

Take It Further

This week after you have spent some quiet time with Jesus and you come across a prayer request on social media, type out a prayer and send.
If someone has a need, offer to pray aloud.

_____

_____

_____

Marie West Wife, mom, grandma, pastor, and BTG missions advisor now living the good life in a real log cabin in God's country in northern Minnesota.

The No-Good, Very Bad Day

Kristin Demery

The Lord is my shepherd, I lack nothing.

Psalms 23:1 (NIV)

The day had been—by any measure—a terrible day. I found out a mold outbreak would require an extensive renovation in our upper level, an exterminator needed to be called for "mice tunnels" in the attic (if that doesn't sound ominous, I don't know what does), a bid for an outdoor project came in at double the expected cost, and my credit card was stolen online. All in one day.

But as I readied for bed, I couldn't help but feel like it was actually a pretty good day.

After dinner, our family savored a snack-filled subscription box we'd received in the mail and ended the evening by watching a kids' movie. As I snuggled up with my 6-year-old on the couch, I savored the moment. The way she laced her small fingers through my own as they rested on the cozy blanket. How the tips of her soft hair tickled my face as she twirled a section round and round her finger. The way she leaned into me, her little body curled into mine.

Those moments of sweetness were just the reminder I needed that life can be both hard and good. As Christians, our contentment is not tied to our current circumstances. In Philippians 4, Paul writes about finding contentment despite facing hardships:

> *Not that I am speaking of being in need, for I have learned in whatever situation I am to be content. I know how to be brought low, and I know how to abound. In any and every circumstance, I have learned the secret of facing plenty and hunger, abundance and need. I can do all things through him who strengthens me.*

> *Philippians 4:10–13, ESV*

Our contentment is not tied to places or things; it's always tied to Jesus. He alone provides the strength we need to face each day.

The Greek word that Paul uses for being content is *autarkes*, which means entirely self-sufficient. "*Autarkeia* was the highest aim of Stoic ethics . . . a state of mind in which a man was absolutely independent of all things and of all people" (*Barclay's Daily Study Bible*). The key difference, according to Barclay, was that the Stoic was self-sufficient—but Paul was God-sufficient.

As Psalm 23:1 reminds us, "The Lord is my shepherd, I lack nothing." (NIV) Because of the power of God at work in our life, we already have all we need. God's abundant life is one in which our sufficiency is found in him.

Though our lives aren't defined by our circumstances, they are often refined by them. And when the hard days come, we can find comfort—and even contentment—in knowing that we're never alone, no matter what we face. God already has all that we need.

Prayer

Jesus, may we choose to remember that you are enough. You're bigger than our hardest days and worst circumstances. Help us to remember that—in you—we have all that we need. May we find the contentment we seek in you and your holy Word. Amen.

Take it Further

Do you believe that God can provide all that you need? Why or why not?

_____

_____

_____

How can claiming contentment in the way that Paul did help us to seek out God's goodness even when circumstances feel difficult?

_____

_____

_____

Kristin Demery's career in journalism set her up to publish her own stories of living this wild, precious life. She now is an author of seven truth-telling books, including the latest *One Good Word a Day,* and part of a trio of writers collectively known as The Ruth Experience. Kristin served as a newspaper and magazine editor and her work has been featured in a variety of publications, including USA Today. She still works behind the scenes as an editor for others while writing her own series on kindness, friendship, and living with intention.

Prayer Flips the Script

Kasha Jankowski

Darkness covers the earth, and total darkness the peoples;
but the Lord will shine over you,
and His glory will appear over you.

Isaiah 60:2 (CSB)

In the past year, I have had the privilege of partnering and supporting the Love This City outreach in the Twin Cities area, based out of Substance Church. A ministry called Manna Market supplies the outreach with food we then use to feed the local community, using large quantities of both fresh and non-perishable produce.

My role is to pray and intercede for those who receive those goods, as well as those who volunteer on a regular basis. This wasn't always my "gig." But this scripture has been stamped on my heart from the day I committed my life to the Lord:

The Spirit of the Sovereign Lord is on me, because the LORD
has anointed me to bring good news to the poor. He has sent
me to comfort the brokenhearted and to proclaim that captives
will be released and prisoners will be set free. To tell those who
mourn that the time of the Lord's favor has come, and with it,

the day of God's anger against their enemies. To all who mourn,
he will give a crown of beauty for ashes and joyous blessing
instead of mourning, festive praise instead of despair.

Isaiah 61:1–3 (NLT)

I wrestled and struggled with this scripture for years, knowing full well that this was a prophecy about Jesus yet feeling as if it was spoken specifically to me. In my mind, claiming a Scripture as my own felt blasphemous, so I tucked it away for a long time.

It wasn't until the pandemic hit that the Lord brought it again to my mind. Although my feeling of inadequacy rose up again, I decided it was not going to stop me this time. I had just enough faith and spiritual maturity to back me up. Instead of dwelling on my perceived weaknesses, I stepped out in faith and began to simply show up. I was willing to be used in whatever capacity was needed, and that is how I ended up in prayer ministry.

On a weekly basis, I watched volunteers set up and tear down this "store" in the middle of a big, open space. I saw guests who walked timidly into the church but gained courage and strength with each step. From the welcome and registration team through all the different stations with items to choose from, each guest was treated with kindness and genuine love. Oftentimes, they'd approach the prayer "table" last, where I got the honor of speaking and praying with them.

Even though I quickly realized that prayer is often overlooked, underestimated, and misunderstood, I believe great things come because of it. Each time we bow our heads in prayer, each time our hearts line up and surrender to his redeeming love, God shows up! It is at this moment that a holy exchange happens—as we bring him our brokenness, failures, fears, and needs, he flips the script and gives us instantaneous hope or peace. A lot of times when we see a change in our present circumstances, we begin to view moments of prayer as divine opportunities for our good! God is so much greater than our present troubles.

God's faithfulness is evident through both individuals and in our ministry. We are never short of volunteers and have never run out of food to give away to our guests. God's arm is never too short to help those in need. Even if the need is within you to release God's living Word, have faith!

> *Believe me when I say that I am in the Father and the Father is in me; or at least believe   on the evidence of the works themselves. Very truly I tell you, whoever believes in me will do the work I have been doing, and they will do even greater things than these, because I am going to the Father. And I will do whatever you ask in my name, so that he may be glorified in the Son."*
>
> *John 14:12,13 (NIV)*

Prayer

Thank you Lord, that your Word—once spoken—does not return void. It accomplishes what you intend for it to do. Thank you for choosing us to be your vessels, bringing your good news to a hurting world. Help us to carry your light into the dark places where you wish to shine, stewarding and sharing your gift with all.

Take It Further

Is there a scripture or truth that God had sealed in your heart? Perhaps he wants you to be the agent who carries out and shares this revelation with others. Write out your next step and invite a friend to keep you accountable.

_____

_____

_____

Kasha Jankowski loves being alive in the Lord. She shares God's heart with anyone who will give her their attention. Vibrant, energetic, and extremely joyful, Kasha brings God's sparkle everywhere she goes. She enjoys people, treats every day as an adventure, and likes to think of shopping as a treasure hunt.

Day 31

Always His Daughter

Nancy Holte

Gray hair is a crown of glory; it is gained in a righteous life.

Proverbs 16:31 (ESV)

Over the past year, I've been struggling with knowing my purpose. Last summer, I qualified for Medicare, which is great for many reasons and horrible because it means I'm kind of old. Because of that age thing and the fact that I go to church where I'm in the minority when it comes to age groups, I had started to feel kind of purposeless and washed-up, as though I had nothing to contribute anymore. My energy level certainly does not help me keep up. Did you know that everything takes longer when you get older? It's annoying.

But recently one of the elders at our church, Keith, came up to me after the service with his wife and asked if he could talk to me. In the past, when Keith has come to talk to me, it's because he has some encouragement from the Lord to share with me, so I look forward to whatever he has to say. It may seem odd to you that the Lord would tell someone else to pass along a message, but God knows we don't always listen well when he speaks to us—especially when his words are encouraging. Maybe it's not that way for you, but even though I know God loves me, I more often than not expect words of correction from God. That's probably because I'm so busy beating myself up for "not doing things right."

When Keith approached me, I wasn't surprised that he had something to say, but I was amazed at his message. He told me that God wanted me to know that even though I'm in the "gray" years (well hidden, thanks to monthly visits to my hairstylist), God still has plans to use me. I'm still significant in the Church. *Seriously? Had Keith been reading my mail?*

Keith's message was encouraging, but it also told me one very important thing: God sees me. He is actively working in my life and knows when I'm struggling. God doesn't want me to waste time having an "I'm so old" pity party. He wants me to use the gifts, talents, and experience that I've acquired to speak into the lives of younger women.

Genesis 16 describes the story of Hagar, the servant to Sarai, Abram's wife. Though God had promised Abram that he would have a son, it didn't happen for a long time. Sarai decided to "help" God by suggesting that Abram sleep with her servant, Hagar. This plan was a colossal disaster. Hagar got pregnant and Sarai got jealous and mean, so Hagar ran away to the wilderness.

Hagar was alone, scared, and in desperate need of some love. But then God showed up. Hagar had an encounter with an angel of the Lord who encouraged her to go back to Sarai. Because of this interaction, Hagar felt seen. She even named the well she was sitting by *Beer-lahai-roi*, which means "well of the Living One who sees me."

Like Hagar, my friend's message from God helped me feel seen. God sees me, cares for me, and still wants to use me for his glory. I'm not an old, washed-up has-been. Instead, I'm at a point in life where God can use me in different—but equally important—ways. While this current season of my life is a new chapter, God already has it written and it is greater than anything that comes my way. He cares about me today, tomorrow, and always.

Prayer

Dear Jesus, please remind me that you always see me. You don't walk away only to come back and find me in a huge mess of my own creation. You are always with me, and you are faithful. Thank you for showing me your love so clearly. Amen.

Take It Further

Are you able to "hear" God speaking to you? Has he ever given you a message that would encourage someone else? Did you pass it along, or were you afraid you might not say it correctly?

_____

_____

_____

How has God shown you lately that he sees you?

_____

_____

_____

Nancy Holte is a wife, mom, grandmother, author, humorist, and encourager who loves to encourage women in their faith walk. Nancy loves to travel, take pictures, and read—especially by the ocean. You can find her on Instagram, Facebook, and at www.nancyholte.com.

Feature Devotional

Andi Andrew is a speaker at Bridging the Gap's 2021 Thrive Conference. She is a wife, mom, pastor, author, speaker, and founder of She Is Free. Andi loves to rally people to the cause of Christ and see them awaken fully to the freedom they have in Him. Andi is the co-founder and co-pastor with her husband, Paul, of the multi-site Liberty Church, which was established in 2010. In 2015 she launched the She is Free Conference, in order to equip women to find freedom, strength, and wholeness in spirit, soul, and body. A frequent speaker all over the world, she and Paul have four children and live in Brooklyn, NY. Learn more: andiandrew.com.

1000+ Little Conversations

Andi Andrew

Parenting is 1000+ little conversations, apologies, cuddles, tears, laughter, and every mundane moment in between. Sometimes uncomfortable, sometimes beautiful, sometimes hilarious, sometimes heartbreaking.

In just the matter of one week, I was asked by our 8-year-old, "What's a condom?" "What is masturbation?" and "What is adultery?" Yes, all in one week, because we live in the real world where condoms hang on the walls of the Public Health Department, and humor on TV shows alludes to masturbation, and adultery—well, we were doing family discipleship and breaking down Proverbs 7, so we opened that door. Can I just say, though, that it was a good week in my mind. I love that we had all of those conversations as a family—in the car, on the couch, and at the dinner table—together. It wasn't awkward. It was appropriate, honest, and free of shame.

As parents, we've got to do whatever we can to connect with our children, and not just on hot topics. Really connect. Heck, even as I was writing this article, one of my kids came in, sat on my bed, and started talking about nothing and everything. At first, in my mind, I thought, "Buddy, can you see I'm writing here?" Then I internally repented, shut my laptop, and listened to him. I asked questions and enjoyed the precious 15 minutes that he chose to come in, connect with me, sit at the foot of my bed, and talk.

If I've learned anything, it's that we cannot let devices and screens win the battle for their affection (or ours, for that matter), because when they're older and leave our homes, they will ask a device for its opinion instead of showing up to family dinner to hear yours.

Build bridges. Find out what they're interested in and ask questions about it, even if you don't get it. Say you're sorry, not "I'm sorry you felt . . . " Don't apologize for their feelings, apologize for your actions—it teaches them to own their stuff, too. Put the intentional time in the calendar to go on a walk with them, grab a hot chocolate, or shop for an outfit. Ask them to go get groceries with you and let them pick the playlist in the car, hold their hand if they still let you, and just take it all in.

Sit at the dinner table together as many times a week as you can. At our dinner table, we talk about politics, sexuality, racism, sex, marriage, Jesus, farts, body parts, video games, friendship, scripture, feelings, highs and lows of the day, and everything in between—nothing is off-limits. It's at the table, on the couch, sitting on the floor, in the corridor, or at the foot of your bed where 1000+ little conversations happen. Where 1000+ little seeds are sown that will grow into something beautiful.

ACKNOWLEDGEMENTS

A devotional book with 27 authors doesn't come together without a team to help bring it to fruition. Special thanks to the women who dedicated countless hours ensuring the book would be a success, including project manager Bri Slegh and editors Diane Shirk, Kristin Demery, and Jonna Meidal. All glory to God—he is greater.